LAKE DISTRICT FOLK

LAKE DISTRICT FOLK

W. R. MITCHELL

FONTHILL

Dedicated to David and Janet

Fonthill Media Language Policy

Fonthill Media publishes in the international English language market. One language edition is published worldwide. As there are minor differences in spelling and presentation, especially with regard to American English and British English, a policy is necessary to define which form of English to use. The Fonthill Policy is to use the form of English native to the author. W. R. Mitchell was born and educated in Skipton, North Yorkshire and lived in Giggleswick, North Yorkshire, until his death in 2015; therefore British English has been adopted in this publication.

Fonthill Media Limited
Fonthill Media LLC
www.fonthillmedia.com
office@fonthillmedia.com

First published in the United Kingdom 2015

British Library Cataloguing in Publication Data:
A catalogue record for this book is available from the British Library

Copyright © W. R. Mitchell 2015

ISBN 978-1-78155-507-1

Typeset in 10pt on 13pt Minion Pro
Printed and bound by CPI Group (UK) Ltd, Croydon, CR0 4YY

Contents

An Introduction   7

1   Local Folk   15

2   On the Fells   18

3   Birds and Beasts   23

4   Delmar and Josephina Banner, Artist and Sculptress   25

5   Clara Boyle, Old Ways of Life   28

6   Reverend G. Bramwell Evans, Romany of the BBC   29

7   Donald Campbell, High Speed on Water   32

8   Lady Anne Clifford, Last of Her Line   33

9   W. G. Collingwood, Links with Ruskin   35

10 Peter Delap, Doctor and Deerologist   37

11 Edward Elgar, His Lakes Overture   39

12 Tissie Fooks, Life in the Rusland Valley   42

13 Bill Grant, Forest and Theatre   45

14 Leslie Grisedale, Shap Fell   48

15 Eric Halsall, *One Man and His Dog*   49

16 Joseph Hardman, Prime Photographer   50

17 W. Heaton Cooper, Artist and Climber   52

18 Herdwick Men and the Native Sheep   55

19 John Hind, Tales from Borrowdale   61

20	William Hully, a Horse Man	64
21	Thomas Longmire, Takking Hod	65
22	Harriet Martineau, a Neighbour of Wordsworth	66
23	Norman Nicholson, Books and Plays	69
24	John Peel, Huntsman and a Song	72
25	Beatrix Potter, Her Life at Far Sawrey	74
26	Arthur Ransome, *Swallows and Amazons*	79
27	Canon Rawnsley, Watchdog of the Lakes	82
28	Will Ritson, the Complete Dalesman	85
29	Cedric Robinson, Queen's Guide to the Sands	87
30	John Robinson, the White House	91
31	H. W. Schneider and the Steam Yacht *Esperance*	93
32	W. T. Shaw, a Miner's World	96
33	Short Brothers, Boats that Flew	98
34	Graham Sutton, a Writer at Dancing Beck	100
35	Alfred Wainwright, Fell Walker Extraordinary	102
36	Robert Walker, a Wonderful Man	111
37	Hugh Walpole, Author of *Herries Chronicle*	112
38	John Wesley and Methodism	114
39	Jonty Wilson, a Shoer of Horses	115
40	William Wordsworth, the Real Man	118
41	Mardale, a Lost Village	125
	Epilogue	128

An Introduction

I was for many years the editor of *Cumbria,* a popular magazine that is concerned with Lake District life and industry. The magazine, originally owned by Lakeland youth hostellers, was transferred to Harry J. Scott, editor of the *Dalesman* magazine. I became 50 per cent of the editorial staff. The slogan was 'put people before things'. I had already done this for many years for the *Dalesman*.

The house in which both magazines were edited was at Clapham, which editorially was a border village. Driving an old car towards the main road, I would turn left for Yorkshire and right for the Lake District! For over half a century I chatted with a host of Lakeland folk who had exciting tales to recall about past days, when the district was a homely area with lots of native folk. I also gleaned the views of a scattering of newcomers interested in many in aspects of local life. This was a wonderful way to earn a living and I count myself privileged to have done so. Outside work hours, and more recently, I had the good fortune to make many visits to the Lake District for a day walking in the fells. I became a member of an energetic quartet of walkers amusingly named the 'Geriatric Blunderers'. Others were Bob Swallow, Stan Field and Colin Pomfret. In the words of Rodgers and Hammerstein, we climbed every mountain and forded every stream—or 'beck', as it is known locally. We adopted the motto, 'you name it, we've been lost on it'.

My early journeys in Lakeland were by motorbike, bus or train. Then I acquired an old Ford car and every journey became an adventure. As I drove down Borrowdale on an especially wet day I had a sinking feeling and, looking down, saw the passing road through a gap in the floor! A Keswick joiner removed the seats, re-flooring the car with creosoted wood.

A number of meetings were repeated on further occasions and I had the pleasure of developing many good friendships. I became a personal friend of Alfred Wainwright, the fell-walker who recorded his many Lakeland walks in hand-written and drawn form. Over many years the 'Geriatric Blunderers' covered all his walks and his celebrated Coast-to-Coast route twixt St Bees and Robin Hood's Bay. I did not complete it in the accepted way; I developed heart trouble at around half way and was whipped off to hospital to have medical attention! The walk was completed in two sections. You won't find that way recommended in Wainwright's guides!

I was always determined to live up to Harry Scott's mantra and put people before things. I relied on my shorthand skills to keep up in the early days but the purchase

The 'Geriatric Blunderers'. From left: Bill Mitchell, Stan Field, Bob Swallow and Colin Pomfret.

of a basic and inexpensive tape recorder made the job much easier. Decades on I have acquired a mountain of tapes, not only on the Lake District but also on the Yorkshire Dales and Lancashire. In the last two or three years some have been digitised and they tell me that they can be found on the web in my W. R. Mitchell Archive! I've not quite mastered the art of surfing on the internet, tending to rely on family members to point things out for me! There is now a mass of information about the whims and fancies of old-time Lakelanders. Much of my interviewing was carried out in my own time and with Harry's approval.

Some of the voices recall wonderful memories about figures who helped to make the Lake District prominent. The daily life of Beatrix Potter, for instance, was recalled by several people who had known her. An old man who had been her shepherd was living alone at a cottage at Far Sawrey. I used to see him in the window and eventually decided to knock on the door and ask him if I could have a chat; he appreciated the company. Josephina Banner, an elderly sculptress, talked about her artwork and recalled the day when, with her artist husband Delmar, she visited Beatrix's home. They knocked on the door. Eventually the patter of footsteps in the passage beyond hinted at her approach. The door was slowly opened—there stood Beatrix, fully clad and with a tea-cosy on her head!

Another mighty literary figure of the area was Arthur Ransome. I was permitted to enter the farm outbuilding where Ransome typed the text of what became *Swallows and*

Amazons, a book about children for children. On the music side, it was not generally known that Edward Elgar, one of our best-known composers, and his wife enjoyed Lakeland holidays. They visited various parts of the region. Elgar's love of the North Country had deepened during visits to Charles William Buck, a medical doctor whose practice was based around Giggleswick in the Yorkshire Dales. Elgar and Buck first met when Buck attended a medical conference at which Elgar, conducting an orchestra, invited Buck to join. Elgar enjoyed visits to Buck's home in Giggleswick; they shared a love of music while walking in limestone country or occupying seats in the doctor's horse-drawn wagonette. Elgar was to provide one of my journalistic life highlights when I was to discover some original, hand-written, signed and dated compositions by the great man. This is one of many joyful memories that will emerge from the pages of this book.

There have been many fascinating encounters. Doreen Wallace, authoress, spoke to me about her exile and return to the Lake District. She had acquired a house called Kirkfell, fairly well up beside the Whinlatter Pass. She gloried when, after shopping in Cockermouth, she walked or rode back home. The road she followed led into 'an ever-narrowing valley choked with mountains; and if the sun shines, the mountains are so rocky that they flash and gleam like cut jewels'.

Edward Jeffrey, who for many years provided watercolour pictures for the cover of *Cumbria* magazine, plus lots of line drawings for text pages, had a charming old-world studio in converted stable buildings at Ravenstonedale. After an art career interrupted by service in the Army during the First World War and a false start as a bookkeeper in industry, he launched himself into commercial art. When Edward was invited by a London publisher to devise a figure that might be loved by children, he created a podgy character called Toby Twire. This was an active little pig wearing red rompers. There were many variations on original themes, including inn signs and greetings cards. Edward was already widely known when I requested him to provide the magazine with artwork showing people and places relevant to the Lake District.

W. A. Poucher photographed my favourite Lakeland view—that of Sphinx Rock, Great Gable, with a glimpse of Wastwater and a gleam from the Irish Sea. Many visitors to the Lake District find a journey to remote Wasdale Church a great experience. The road from Gosforth heads for 4 miles between shapely fells, and offers a view of a trinity of mountains—Great Gable, Yewbarrow and Lingmell—which appear on the emblem of the Lake District National Park.

I wrote a script about John Peel, huntsman, for local radio. Carlisle was at that time an outpost of BBC Newcastle. In the Civic Hall at Carlisle I listened to Men of the Fells as, lustily, they recorded the John Peel song for the programme.

So many interesting folk from such a small area. The distance from Ennerdale, in the west, to Shap, in the east, is 40 miles. An energetic person might cross it in twenty-four hours. Like its people, the land is full of character. I explored a region of infinite variety. Radiating from a rugged dome is a radial drainage pattern, created when old river valleys and fault lines were eroded, then smoothed by the slow but remorseless action of

Farmers at Eskdale Show in 1963. (Drawing by E. Jeffrey)

glaciers. John Ruskin, an eminent Victorian who spent part of his life at Brantwood, on the shores of Coniston Water, had a splendid view of the fell known as the Old Man. To Ruskin, 'mountains are the beginning and end of all natural scenery'. The Lake District resembles a wheel. Dales extend like spokes from the central hub—a cluster of high fells. The oldest rocks are sedimentary. Five hundred million years ago the area which is now called Lakeland was underwater, receiving silt from great rivers. Then a volcano flared, pouring out lava and tufts. The landscape set in terror. When the rocks were formed, cracked and folded, they were shaped by glacial ice.

Lakeland stone is famous world-wide, and the area is patterned by the distinctive drystone walls, the means by which pieces of land have been separated for generations. The construction method has changed little over the years. These walls do not have a dab of mortar. Each is two walls in one, side-by-side, the whole tapering slightly, being bound together with 'throughs' that extended from one side of the wall to the other. The average height is between 4 feet 6 inches and 5 feet. A farmer might devote three weeks of every year to their maintenance. Material for building was usually freestone, secured at small, handy quarries, and slate. Stone for the walls running to the fell-tops, enclosing the intakes, might have to be sledded. The sleds would have been drawn by sure-footed ponies known as Galloways. Valley stone is not the best walling material, being mainly cobbles from the river—rounded by the action of water. Felltop stone still has an edge to it. Most gaps appear in the thaw after frosty weather. An Eskdale farmer once told me, 'When you see a wall shutter in a hard spell you know it's going to thaw.'

Such walls, with their durable capping of topstones (also known as 'cam-stones'), provided good shelter for sheep and other creatures and, properly built, could last a lifetime. The creatures might lig (lie) on the lee side when wind and rain were in an uncomfortable partnership. Hog-holes were left so that if necessary sheep might pass from one grazing area to another. If the farmer wished to confine sheep to a specific area, such holes were covered by slabs of slate.

Farming in the upper dales evolved in response to a rocky terrain, to a weepy climate and to a long winter. Lakeland had no permanent snow cover, but snow might 'powder' the tops on many days of the year. The poet Wordsworth loved those 'bold burst[s] of sunshine, the descending vapours, wandering lights and shadows and the invigorating torrents and waterfalls with which broken weather, in a mountainous region, is accompanied'.

The old roads of Lakeland meandered amiably about the landscape for many centuries but, at a time of change, the M6 swept grandly northwards through the Lune Gorge and over the heights of Shap to Carlisle. The heart of Lakeland became approachable via a branch of the M6—the Kendal bypass—leading into a much improved road to Windermere. The locals have now been joined by many thousands of visitors and others who have made the area their second home. There has been much for the Cumbrian folk to take on board. As one said to me, 'Life's all of a splutter'.

Life as I first experienced it as editor of *Cumbria* magazine in the 1950s had simplicity and stability, enacted against a background of lakes, tarns and shapely fells. I frequently

Raven, a craft in the spectacular setting of Ullswater.

left my desk and office to wander where the spirit moved me, chatting with whoever seemed interesting. Natural beauty abounds in the Lake District; at the head of Ullswater, the fells appear to spring directly from the water, as they do in the fjords of Norway.

The Lake District National Park, designated in the first year of my editorship, had become the largest of its type, having an area extending to 880 square miles. Three counties—Cumberland, Westmorland and Lancashire—possessed wedge-shaped slices of the Lakeland 'cake'. The ways of life between the fell ranges had not changed greatly for many years. There was a sense of isolation. Local life charmed me with its quaintness.

In this book I have picked out some of the many characters who have been part of my journey. With those who pre-deceased me there is usually a link as I will have either spoken to those who knew them or I have been allowed access to their world. The great names like Wordsworth and Potter have undoubtedly played their part in popularising the Lakes, but the real charm and character lies in the ordinary, everyday Cumbrian folk; their recollections have enriched my life. Homespun philosophy characterises every conversation and provides amusing and thought-provoking lines, not least when the voice is comparing present and past and commenting on the pace of life.

Veteran blacksmith Jonty Wilson had a forge at Kirkby Lonsdale. He remarked sadly that the horse world and old husbandry had passed into the limbo of history. So, too, have many vivid expressions. An old chap summed up his age by remarking, 'I've one foot in t'grave and t'other foot on a banana skin, ready for slipping in.'

When I asked another old chap for his age, he replied: 'I'se eighty-three.' I sought to compliment him by saying, 'You don't look eighty-three.' His reply was a simple, 'Can't help that!' A farmer travelling on a motorised trike, which had 'balloon tyres' and a

Japanese trademark, was taking food 'pellets' and hay to his older Herdwick ewes. He held up one of the pellets and said, 'It's powerful stuff. You could tame lions with it!'

In 1778 a Jesuit priest named Father West wrote the first Lakeland guidebook. It stimulated a trickle of visitors who were keen to experience more about the picturesque outdoors and who had been denied making the Grand Tour of Europe because of war with France. Father West's little book had a reverential air. He recorded 'stations' or viewpoints, a notion which may have been inspired by Stations of the Cross. One of the 'stations' lay to the west of Windermere, with a view across the lake to volcanic hills grouped to the north of Ambleside, a focal town that would become noted for its distinctive Bridge House. This was not built by a Scotsman who was keen to avoid ground rent—it was a prominent feature in the garden of the former Ambleside Hall.

West's modest effort has spawned a tidal wave. Step into any Cumbrian book shop and you will find a host of guides, written from every angle and produced in a variety of ways. The audio and the visual stand alongside more traditional methods. They have helped make the area fully accessible; that is good, but I am glad that many of my sixty years or so took me off the beaten track, out of prime holiday and weekend time, and allowed me to enjoy the tranquillity and the people of this very special part of the country.

A roadside sign in Kentmere.

Acknowledgements

Photographs are from the W. R. Mitchell collection. Many thanks go to David, my son, and Janet, my daughter, for their help in preparing this book. Also, thank you to all the Lakeland folk that I have met over the years—it has been a delight and a privilege to have known you.

A Note from the Author's Children

Dad died on 7 October 2015, after a short illness. Two days before he passed away we told him that the final manuscript for *Lake District Folk* had been sent to the publishers. His mantra throughout his journalistic career had been 'People Before Things', so it is appropriate that this book focuses on folk; it is also appropriate that it is set in an area he knew so well. He leaves a remarkable legacy, with over 200 books to his name.

David and Janet

1

Local Folk

Folk have lived in the Lake District for many centuries, and there have been some significant periods in the area's history—a subject which has fascinated many a historian. A local friend called such research 'pokin' abaht in t'long deeard past'. The Celtic presence is most evident in names given to natural features like rivers and hills. River names are short and somewhat sharp—among them are Kent, Leven, Irt, and Esk. Celts named Skiddaw, Blencathra, Helvellyn and Maiden Moor, the 'maiden' being derived from *myddyn* (middle). Sheep-counting numerals, a curious survival from Celtic times, acquired a form that began *Yan, Tan, Tethra, Methra, Pip*. Each word probably represented a group of five sheep.

With Hadrian's Wall stretching west to east at the top end of the area, the Roman presence is assured. Towards the end of last century a farmhand sat down to have a smoke while shepherding on Mallerstang Edge, overlooking the Eden. There was a flat stone near his feet. He kicked it away, and underneath was a hoard of 128 Roman coins.

At Wasdale Head, a car park lies not too far from a little church that had been nameless for 450 years. In 1977, a Bishop of Carlisle put it under the patronage of St Olaf—the man who converted Norwegians to Christianity. Wasdale, in its long history, had Norse connections. I was especially fond of learning about the people in what was known as 't'owd days'. Among the oldest would be the time when St Bega, a legendary seventh-century Irish saint, accompanied by a small band of nuns, landed on the coast. Their object was to establish a religious house. The local lord, asked for a grant of land, said as a jocular remark that they could have whatever land was covered with snow on Midsummer Day. The nun's prayers—and climatic vagaries—led to a snowfall on a wide area. The site of the monastery founded by Bega became widely known as St Bees. The early settlers were hunters. The culinary jackpot would be capturing a red deer, which—apart from being a huge source of protein—yielded antlers and bone for domestic use, in addition to skins with which to make simple tents. Arrow heads of this period have been located on High Wray. Much later, Norse terms began to pepper the district, forming the language of topography.

Farm life became organised when the great abbeys of the twelfth and thirteenth centuries acquired land and established granges. The sheep farms of Furness Abbey were known as *herdwycks*, a name subsequently adopted for the local breed of sheep. The Cistercian monks clothed themselves in white cloth (un-dyed wool). Their *vaccaries* (dairy farms) became features of the dales. The fell country became an extensive sheep walk.

What became known as the Romantic Age blossomed between 1760 and 1820. People with taste, money and leisure responded to a cult known as the Picturesque. Earlier that century some of them found the scenery of the Lake District wild, barren and frightful. They were awestruck by the Pennine escarpment as viewed from the Eden Valley. By the middle of the century, artists, poets and tourists were sharing in the discovery of the Lake Counties as portrayed in words and also paintings that were exhibited.

Wealthy landowners changed or beautified their estates, giving them an appeal to a visitor with a Romantic disposition. Shooting pheasants that had been bred from Asian jungle fowl were available for sport. A demand arose for rhododendrons, ideal for providing cover for game; they helped to adorn a natural scene. Also created during this period were The Nunnery Walks on the eastern bank of the Eden, which gushed through a gorge between red-stone cliffs.

During the Romantic period viewpoints were recommended. Thomas Gray (1769) went as far as Grange, hastening in silence, fearful that, as in the Alps, the 'agitation of the air' would dislodge rocks from the crags. In that same year Thomas Pennant found pleasure in Windermere, the most extensive lake. He landed and dined at what he termed *Boulnes* (Bowness). It was, he noted, anciently called *Winander*. Pennant dined on 'the most delicate trout and perch'. Char, which were plentiful in the lake, were of a size 'superior to those in Wales'. Viewpoints were recommended for a visitor who might use a Claude glass, turning his back on the view, which was reflected in the glass and might be framed to fit a stilted notion. I was amused by a poem about Coniston Old Man that was penned by a Victorian writer named A. C. Gibson. Here's the first verse:

Old man! Old man! Your sides are brant,
And fearfully hard to climb;
My limbs are weak and my breath is scant,
So I'll rest me here and rhyme.

Left: Ancient graves; a stone circle near Askham.

Opposite: Joss Naylor (right) with his wife and a Wasdale neighbour at Wasdale Show.

In the old days, farming families were self-sufficient. They produced a few items of food and they clothed themselves with wool from their sheep, a mixture of white and black wool creating a type of cloth known as *hodden grey*. John Peel, the huntsman, wore 'a coat so gray'—not 'gay', as in the popular song. Old-time Lakeland farming families usually had *poddish* (porridge) for breakfast. It was thick, made in a pan over an open fire, stirred with a stick called a *thible* and served in basins. A diner must clean up his basin—the same vessel might later hold a drink of tea. At Skelwith Bridge I heard that 'they set t'pan in t'middle o' t'table. You could help yourself'.

Porridge for breakfast was generally supplemented with bacon and egg. The midday meal usually included puddings: rice, sago or a variety of steamed creations. At a farm in Mardale they 'had bread and butter and jam. There was home-made cake—but not much o' that!' Supper at a Lakeland farm usually began between 6 and 6.30 p.m. If a farmer kept a goodly number of ducks, some of the new-laid eggs might appear on the table.

Not surprisingly for such a well-established and distinctive area, traditions have become embedded in the culture, not least in sporting activity. There has always been a sporting side to Lakeland life; fell running has its roots on the fells of northern Britain, especially those in the Lake District. Joss Naylor was often the man to beat. Born at Wasdale Head in 1936, Naylor combined sheep farming with his love of running and became known as the King of the Fells—or simply 'Iron Man'. None other than Chris Brasher described Naylor as 'the greatest of them all'. Among all the redoubtable fell-running heroes his exploits are legendary, including running over seventy-two Lakeland peaks inside twenty-four hours in 1975.

Young men interested in wrestling used a variety of local terms, including hod, hype, hank, and clicks. From May to October the wrestling fans have congregated at shows to see the lads take hold. This 'grass season' usually ends a Wasdale Head show, after which the sport goes under-cover. The traditional costume for wrestling consists of silk vest and slips, with coloured trunks (often elaborately embroidered) and socks. A wrestling bout is lost by the first wrestler to touch the ground with any part of his body other than his feet.

2

On the Fells

I began fell-walking in the 1950s. It was a time when Wainwright was known only in local government circles at Kendal. 'Cubby' Acland, with a little help, managed a modest number of properties of the National Trust, which is now the major landowner. The Lake District National Park had been designated in May 1951, less than a month after the first park, which was the Peak District. There are many fascinating and spectacular routes across this beautiful countryside. As well as the chance to enjoy bracing air and exercise, each is a walk through history, and it would be difficult to pick out a favourite.

High Street is a name associated with the Romans, who, having constructed some fine roads around the fells, now had to make their presence known among them. The Romans selected the line of an old British trackway—a route which for 12 continuous miles maintains a height of over 2,000 feet. A party of Roman soldiers, setting out from the fort at *Brocavum* (Brougham), near tropical Penrith, headed, doubtless with some foreboding but on remarkably level high ground, for *Galava* (Ambleside). My goodness, the breeze was 'thin' when three of us followed the route taken by Roman troops. We found ourselves on a long, open stretch of ground. The ancient gods may have drawn a curtain of cloud across the sky but the air remained dryish.

The Langdale Pikes, standing at the head of the dale after which they are named, are craggy mountains formed of volcanic tuffs and rhyolite that give them precipitous forms. They break the skyline like a double-headed sphinx and impart to the district a touch of operatic grandeur.

To Wordsworth, glancing back as he strode near Blea Tarn, the Pikes appeared to be standing on tip-toe! Pike o' Stickle (2,325 feet) and Harrison Stickle (2,404 feet) form a twin-turreted profile; completing a trio of shapely 'pikes' is Loft Crag (2,198 feet). Nearby, Gimmer Crag is one of the top rock-climbing venues in the Lake District. Formed from rhyolite, it was pioneered in the early 1880s by Walter Parry Haskett Smith, the father of British rock climbing.

Rock-climbing became popular in Lakeland in around the 1860s. Atkinson, an Ennerdale cooper, challenged the crags when he climbed Pillar Rock by the old west route in 1826. Early climbers wore Norfolk jackets, breeches and long stockings. Nailed boots and hempen rope had been used until the 1920s, when boots gave way to the more sensitive plimsolls. In 1956, when I chatted with Stanley Watson, the tendency was for long ski-trousers and windjammers. Nylon ropes and shoes of hard composition rubber, as worn by Commandos during the war, had become popular.

Langdale Pikes viewed from Little Langdale.

Stanley had done much for mountaineering. In 1930 he founded the British Mountain Guides, and he had a climbing school at Newton Place, in Borrowdale. Stanley's favourite mountain was Great Gable. He pointed out to newcomers that the climbs, facing south, were clean. A climber had the benefit of sunlight. He was unlikely to encounter moss and water. Stanley climbed Kern Knotts blindfolded! He was on Helvellyn with three friends when a blizzard greatly reduced visibility and lasting snow led to much shutting of eyes. Stanley could not believe that such conditions might occur on a little 3,000-foot peak.

Rock-climbing had its lighter moments. In a record book kept at Wasdale Head there were two droll entries—the first simply stated, 'Today I ascended the pillar in three hours and found the rocks very soft.' Scrawled underneath, by a wag, were the words: 'To-day I descended the Pillar in three seconds—and found the rocks very hard.'

Some 4,000 years ago Pike o' Stickle became the setting for Lakeland's first-known industry—a so-called axe factory, where a fine-grain tuff, formed of volcanic dust, was recovered to be sharpened, honed and fitted with a strong shaft. Thus was created the Great Cumbrian Axe. It helped to transform the landscape from forest to grassland. Axe-heads were possibly roughed-out *in situ*, the roughs being taken to sites near the coast, where working conditions were more amenable and there was an abundance of sandstone to give the axes a polish before they were distributed along track-routes to other parts of the country. I realised an old ambition when, with a close friend and with great care, we descended the upper part of a 2,000-feet scree slope to find evidence of the industrial activity. We were in the footsteps of Neolithic man who, by all accounts, was short and none-too-merry, ending—no doubt—with joints locked up through arthritis. The men who sought tuff would be accustomed to climbing on steep paths formed on rocky slopes. They were probably most scared of meeting aggressive members of a rich and diverse fauna. The wildwood of those days would be tenanted by wolves, bears and wild boars. We came across a point at which the screes might be fettled in a shallow cave.

Mining scars later areas of Coniston fells. Copper was mined here from around 1599, possibly even earlier. At the height of production, in the middle of the nineteenth century, no less than 600 people were employed in and around the Coppermines Valley. Most of the present remains date from post-1830. Until the railway opened in 1859 the copper was transported to Greenodd, which then had a thriving little port, shipping from there to St Helens in Lancashire. Here it was turned into copper sheets for sheathing the bottoms of wooden sailing vessels. The decline of the copper mines was rapid. It came about partly from the end of wooden ships and from the exploitation, on a vast scale, of overseas copper beds. There was also an uncreatingly difficult task of pumping water from deep levels in the fell. By 1889 the Coniston labour force consisted of a few dozen men; the mines closed at the turn of the century, though spasmodic attempts to work some of them have taken place.

Bob Swallow and I ticked off Coniston Old Man one summer. By contrast, one of its neighbours, Wetherlam, turned out to be an 'ice-axe job'. Wainwright had likened the 2,502-feet Wetherlam to 'a giant whale surfacing above waves of lesser hills'. If you want spectacular with a hint of trepidation then climb Helvellyn along Striding Edge. The walk usually starts at Glenridding Bridge, near Ullswater. This is definitely one for the experienced walker for it is the most celebrated ridge walk in Lakeland, being not only rocky but very narrow. A climber must have a clear head on a good day. A sweeping ridge leads from Striding Edge to Swirrel Edge. Far below is Red Tarn.

Ullswater from Glenridding Dodd, featuring Colin Pomfret.

Someone assumed that the name Striding Edge came from the necessity of the walker to stride over gaps which, from a distance, resemble the serrated back of a prehistoric reptile. On a misty day there is a spooky appearance. In windy conditions, opt for the lower track. Sir Walter Scott (1805) wrote romantically about the experience in a poem that begins:

> *I climbed the dark brow of the mighty Helvellyn,*
> *Lakes and mountains beneath me gleamed misty and wide;*
> *All was still, save by fits, when the eagle was yelling*
> *And starting around me the echoes replied.*

In my book *After you, Mr Wainwright* I described Helm Crag, above Grasmere, as 'Midget of a Mountain'. Having attained the topmost rock I reached swaggeringly to my rucksack for a celebratory drink of thermos tea. As I drank, a passing raven flicked over on its back, giving me a 'victory roll'.

Another expedition took in Sty Head and Sprinkling Tarn to Esk Hause, which is situated at the hub of the Lakeland wheel. The Hause is arguably the wettest area in Lakeland. A bucket makes the best rain gauge. It was a good day on which to visit Esk Hause, which, with a rainfall of about 185 inches *per annum*, is rarely dry underfoot. We took the track for Stockley Beck and Sty Head Tarn; then it began to rain. The stones beneath our feet, polished by myriad boots, became slippery. We had our first 'butty stop' near Sty Head, with our backs to a large first-aid box. Then we struck off for Sprinkling Tarn. Two lads on mountain bikes were blown to a standstill and had to walk for a while. Colourful blobs on the leesides of boulders by Sprinkling Tarn indicated where walkers had stopped to sup and eat. And so we came to the slanting stretch of grassland known as Esk Hause. It might be termed the Crossroads of Mountain Lakeland—if only the paths crossed. Sitting at the Hause I was aware only of walkers appearing from several directions, some being at the latter stages of an ascent of Scafell Pike, the attic of England.

In its northward progress, the main Lakeland road (A592) cuts through a swathe of Silurian country around Windermere and enters the area of the Borrowdale Volcanics at Ambleside. The transition is visibly abrupt. Smooth rolling hills give way to the craggy mountains. Keswick, northern capital of Lakeland, is so well placed that a visitor might select a walk to suit the current mood. To the north, the fells—composed of Skiddaw slates—are large and rounded. 'Slates' is the wrong term; they are really an assortment of flagstones, shales and mudstones, laid down—as indicated—on the bed of an ancient sea. They formed during the Ordovician period some 480 million years ago. Take a second glance at Skiddaw. It is older than the Alps and the Himalayas! Coleridge, pondering on Skiddaw in 1802, wrote: 'O its fine black head & the bleak air a top of it, with a prospect of mountains all about & about, making you giddy...'

Among my memorable walks was the traverse of the Fairfield Horseshoe. We often kept slightly entertaining reports of our fell-top achievements, so I am able to recall amusing and interesting incidents with some certainty. When we booted-up at Rydal, one member focused his digital camera on the rest, prompting another to remark, 'If we don't smile now, we never will.' I used a camcorder to record faces rather than the backs of heads on the initial climb—Nab Scar.

Having left the shadows of Rydal on a walk that had begun at 9.15, we had to endure rays from a sun that was like a blow-torch. Sunlight brought a gleam to the bracken fronds which, bent back, were beginning to suffer from old age. Foxgloves, brown and forlorn, were like spent rockets. Up, up, up, with pauses to admire the view, which was dramatic when, at 11.20 a.m., we reached a grassy ledge—our Advance Base Camp. We beheld the Danube-blue lake of Rydal with lush fields in the foreground and traffic looking, from this height, like a line of Dinky toys. The path levelled out, then tilted again for the grand assault on Heron Pike. We admired two sheep of indeterminate breed and a pond from which dragonflies emerged to harden their wings and have their brief moment of glory in sunshine. We mustered at the cairn on Heron Pike (2,403 feet). The event was recorded photographically. Cyril made the necessary adjustment to the number of miles on a small hymn board (courtesy of the Catholic Church he attended). We pressed on to Rydal Fell (2,022 feet), flushing four meadow pipits. A throaty croak came from a raven that was 'telling us off'. Then elevenses, with discussion centring on food, mainly types of sandwich. After a long drag we attain Great Rigg Man at 2,513 feet. The top of the cairn teemed with flies. 'Something' bit Terry on the back of his neck.

We attained Fairfield, the highpoint, at 2,862 feet. Its 'fair-fieldness' had vanished under boulders and boot-pounded earth. We heard the distant throbbing of the blades of a Chinook helicopter. It was later seen hovering, shining bright when it caught the eye of the sun. Animal life consisted of one Herdwick sheep. It was lunchtime. The view took in a valley that, fancifully, was something of the shape of a Viking longboat. A sheep got down on its fore knees to nibble at an especially green patch of vegetation.

We moved on to the rockscape of Hart Crag (2,698 feet). No self-respecting deer would be found here. Progress was now on ankle-wrecking rockscape, enlivened when we met a Geordie who, in his voice, had retained the rich tone of his native speech. During the descent, the party split into two. We descended to the verdant bowl of Rydal Park—and, nine-and-a-quarter hours after setting off, we regained our cars.

Cross Fell, the highest point on the Pennines, is on a popular long-distance walk known as the Pennine Way. A pilgrim with a car might drive to the small village of Knock, at the foot of the northern Pennines, and use the first part of a cul-de-sac road that serves the radome establishment on Great Dun Fell. The rest of the journey to the Pennine Way is to be undertaken on your two feet. Now walk over Little Dun Fell and ascend to the bare, windswept acres of Cross Fell (2,930 feet). I can recall when one used to 'splosh' across marshy ground. Now much of the felltop stretch has been stone-flagged.

Birds and Beasts

I have had a lifelong interest in wildlife, and the Lake District is a veritable treasure chest. Wild creatures that inhabit the hinterland range in size from the goldcrest, the smallest British bird, to a red stag, the largest native mammal. Names on the map hint at the old-time avifauna—Eagle Crag, Glead Howe (Hill of the Kite), Falcon Crag. There are several Raven Crags. Activity aplenty has transfixed ornithologists over the years. All the birds mentioned in the place names, except the kite, nested here in recent times. A red kite was, however, seen near Wastwater. It was an exciting time for bird-watchers when two golden eagles had their nest in one of the offshoot valleys of Mardale. I have seen a dotterel on Cross Fell, high spot of the Pennines.

The fell country or the lonely hills support a sparse bird population. A trio of big birds—peregrine falcon, buzzard and raven—have nested on the crags. The greylag was re-established as a wild-nesting species after several centuries following the introduction of Scottish birds by way of a reserve in the Duddon Valley. Southern woodlands were colonised by the green woodpecker. Ravens hung on in Lakeland despite a considerable increase in the number of walkers and climbers who violated the traditional nesting crags of this and other species. Buzzards re-established themselves in woodland.

Fox-hunting has been a Lakeland sport for many years. The Millom poet, Norman Nicholson, features later in the book, and in my chat with him he showed sympathy for the fox. In his *Portrait of the Lakes* he noted that 'when hounds stream across open fellside or nose up and down a larch wood with a flurry of terriers behind them, I cannot forget the wretched animal with its lungs and heart half-burst even before the teeth get at it'. Nevertheless, he continued, it was not just a social gathering for organised cruelty. 'Foxes have to be kept down somehow and it is at least arguable that hunting is the most practical.'

My favourite mammal is the red deer; it can readily adapt itself to circumstances. Mike, a deer-watcher friend, spent much time on the eastern fells, studying a type of deer that was midway in size between the big woodland reds of Furness and the smaller, leaner stock of the open fells, such as those round Martindale. One summer's day Mike and I walked in a dale that was lacklustre under cloud and must have held a thousand shades of green. The ravens had reared their young and departed. A pair of buzzards circled and mewed over a nest on a cliff-side rowan, where a single well-feathered young bird lay. Two herons rose from the beck. They circled and settled. Mike had 'glassed' herons when feeding. He noticed that voles were consumed immediately but if the bird caught a frog it washed it before it was swallowed! Several hundred red deer were to be found on a little-visited eastern expanse of fell. The stags I observed at close quarters had black noses, well-moistened, with silvery highlights where they caught the light. The world of the red deer is largely one of scent. The animal frequently runs its tongue over its nose to improve its scenting capabilities.

In mid-winter, Lakeland stags are still recovering from the excesses of the rut; they put on weight through grazing and browsing against the lean days of spring and before the first flush of new growth appears on the fellsides. Mike and I, both keen deer-watchers, named some of the stags. Mike chose the name Rasputin for an oldish stag that spent its last days in peace, if not entirely without pain. It might, like some retired colonel, become arthritic.

Studying the wildlife of the Lake District has been a particular source of pleasure to me and some of my featured characters later in the book have done much to help conserve perpetuate a thriving animal and bird population.

My choice of features has no one thing in common other than the fact that they have come into my sixty-year love affair with the Lake District and made a mark on my own life. Most embrace a number of areas including art, music, literature and conservation, but some are genuine one-offs whose individualistic charm has captured my attention at some point between the 1950s and today. They are in alphabetical order so don't read too much into where they are on the list!

Delmar and Josephina Banner, Artist and Sculptress

Delmar and Josephina Banner met during their student days at the Regent Street Polytechnic in London. A frieze I admired in their old farmstead on a fellside in Little Langdale was painted when they were living in Sussex and were homesick for the mountains. 'The Bield', as their three-centuries-old farmstead was called, was named after a word meaning 'shelter', though it was perched high on a fell slope, with a view, across the valley, of a modest tarn and the fell known as Wetherlam. Ancient yews and oaks moderated the fury of a northerly wind.

Delmar and Josephina had known and respected the dalesfolk since the days when they lodged at farms in the district for months on end and ventured out to capture Lakeland in its various moods. Delmar was an artist of the mountain tops. Josephina de Vasconcellos, as she was often known, spent much of her time as a sculptress. She had been born near London. Her father was a Brazilian and mother came from English Quaker stock with Maryport associations.

Josephina had started sculptural work at the age of three. Wandering in the garden, she found some clay under the lawn and began to model it excitedly. When I chatted with her in Little Langdale she recalled the thrill of moulding clay into a bird's nest. Her parents allowed her to leave school when she was fourteen years of age. Her sculptural skills were acquired in the yards of stone masons at the Regent Street Polytechnic, the Royal Academy Schools and through studies in Florence, Paris and Rome.

Despite living in Sussex, the Banners always hoped to settle in the Lake District. The barn at the Bield became their studio. Delmar, though not physically strong, was noted for his paintings of the mountain tops. He spent hundreds of hours at high elevation, where mist sneaked round lichen-patterned rocks and one might hear the gruff voices of ravens. He took food with him on his fell-top excursions but so absorbed was he in art he was inclined to forget it.

Delmar was entranced by the relationship between the solid, sculptural fells and the sea of air in which they swam. He noted:

It is the supreme character of the fells, as the eye tries to grasp them, that they are objects of solid rock, fire-tempered, ice-hewn and enduring through a long time. Yet, also, they are distant, mysterious, swimming in a sea of light and air and light and colour that shifts and dissolves and obscures.

The drawings and colour notes he made out-of-doors were of oil or chalk.

A former bracken loft was used as a Lake District studio. I entered it and viewed Glaramara from the centre of what was called the 'boys' room. A panorama, painted from drawings Delmar made during a seven-hour stint on the summit of Glaramara, formed a frieze around three walls of the room, demonstrating his fine sense of perspective. He had lightly wrapped the Lakeland fells in vapour. The desired matt finish had been obtained by mixing oil paint with petroleum!

Delmar could paint air. Damp Lakeland air held the light in a curious way. 'The identical never recurs,' said the artist. 'Even typically similar conditions may not recur during a whole season or for years. Many of the events of mountain nature that are most worthy of record are past in a few moments.' No day was good or bad. It was simply dry or wet.

When I first met Josephina she was sharing the old farmstead with Delmar. On our next meeting, when Delmar had died, I conversed with her as she sat beside a coal fire in a cosy, white-painted cottage—one of many such cottages in Old Ambleside. I had been invited for tea. Darkness had fallen. Striding down a steepish slope, I glanced through curtainless windows, looking for Josephina. Graceful and elderly, she was sitting by an open fire, not far from a round table laid out for a meal. The furnishings, old and grand, had a Victorian flavour. I had been invited to have tea with her and a mystery guest, who turned out to be W. Heaton Cooper, the artist. We enjoyed the meal and chatted cordially about local affairs.

When I next met Josephina she was aged ninety-one—and still sculpting. She had moved from the lile cottage to a nearby building that served as both studio and living quarters. It was tucked out of sight, behind a high wall, not far from the aforementioned cottage. The large blocks of stone she required for sculpting had been lifted over the wall by mobile crane.

How did she find the strength to do major work? She remarked:

I am quite young inside and old outside. I find that being old is rather like feeling as you do after an operation in hospital. You wonder why you're so weak … It isn't much a matter of strength; it's one of rhythm. I've done this work for many years … It's not a strain; it's just a pleasant exercise.

Josephina did not keep regular hours:

If I go to bed early, it will be about half past one. I wake up at five or six o'clock. If I go to bed late, it will be half past three. And if I go to bed at half past four, it is not worth undressing. I just lie on the bed with something over me—and call it a night. In those cases I wake up about nine.

Recent work had included filling three niches, 20 feet up, at Carlisle Cathedral.

They had never been filled since it was built. The conventional response would have been to represent three saints. The work in the central niche shows Jesus with a baby on His shoulder and a little girl clinging to him. On each side are angels bringing in the kids … The whole thing is linked.

My last encounter with Josephina was equally remarkable. It took place at dusk in Kendal; I had been told that she was living in rooms down one of the yards. The last doorway gave access to a staircase. I knocked on a door and was invited, faintly, to enter. Josephina was lying, fully dressed, on a large four-poster bed. In the room was sparse furnishing and some fine examples of her art and craft. I was allowed to place my tape-recorder on the side of the bed. She recalled the life that she and her dear husband had spent in Little Langdale. Her recollections were so wondrous that, as she spoke, my eyes moistened.

Clara Boyle, Old Ways of Life

Clara Boyle lived at Ambleside, at the heart of the Lake District, and was a living link with some of the pre-1914 notables. A Polish lady, Clara married a diplomat named Henry Boyle. Clara recalled for me the 'old days' when large Victorian houses, set in capacious grounds, were occupied by well-esteemed families. Men ruled the roost (or thought they did). Society women, swaddled in long gowns, gossiped over afternoon tea in houses that swarmed with servants. A horse was master of the dusty road.

On Clara's first visit to Ambleside, in 1911, Nellie Boyle—her future mother-in-law—had tea made for Fraulein von Grimm, who was to Clara 'a stout, elderly lady of at least forty-five'. She had resided in England for about a quarter of a century and was noted as the sister of the celebrated Grimm brothers, who had given to the world what Clara described as 'the somewhat gruesome Grimm's fairy-tales'.

Clara became friendly with Violet Wordsworth, great-granddaughter of the poet and the last of the family to reside at Rydal Mount, Grasmere. Violet had, somewhat appropriately, violet-blue eyes; at Rydal Mount her dress, carpets and curtains were chosen to match them. Clara remembered Violet's funeral, which took place on an autumn day in 1919. The coffin, borne down the aisle at St Mary's Church, Ambleside, was followed by her husband—'a shrivelled, pathetic little man … crippled and dying of pernicious anaemia'.

Clara did not restrict her memories to the 'nobs'. She was fond of recalling Old Barham, the last Vicar of Mardale. When she saw him he was old and eccentric, bent double under a heavy load of bracken:

> He wore an old black suit, green with age and discoloured with many stains. He was a man of culture and literary taste but was desperately lonely. His little church was practically deserted. The few families scattered on lonely farms up and down the valley preferred the more genial administrations and human understanding of the Vicar of Bampton, a few miles further north.

She remembered Willie Heelis, solicitor husband of Beatrix Potter. They had been married in 1913. Willie and Clara were in the same folk-dancing group. He looked more like a farmer than a professional man. He helped his wife with the housework, even to curing the hams. Clara, who contributed to *Cumbria* magazine at the time I was Editor, had a clear memory of her meeting with Canon Rawnsley in 1914. This little man, as described by Clara, was stocky, with broad shoulders, broad face and broad, close-cropped beard. He was one of the founders of The National Trust.

Reverend G. Bramwell Evans, Romany of the BBC

In my boyhood I was fascinated by Romany of the BBC—he awakened in me what would become a great interest in the countryside and its wild creatures. A Methodist minister, he called himself Romany because he was born of a gipsy mother. Lakeland was familiar to him. For fourteen years, until 1926, he was a Methodist minister at Carlisle, becoming well-known in the city as the man who organised Sunday-evening services in a local picture house. He led the team who built Central Hall. It was opened free of debt.

When this minister preached, he spoke simply, with stories drawn from the experience of the countryside—and especially memories of regular visits to the Potter family, who lived at Old Parks, a red-sandstone farmhouse at Glassonby, in Edenvale. These farm folk—also Comma, the horse that who drew the Romany caravan, and Raq, an attendant cocker spaniel—helped to give the associated BBC radio programmes a vast following. Raq was also permitted to be with him in the pulpit for a few minutes when he was guest preacher at a Sunday School Anniversary in Wordsworth Street Methodist Church, Penrith.

There was joy for radio listeners in being *Out with Romany*, which was broadcast from Manchester. The series lasted for ten happy years from 1933. Broadcasters were 'uncles' and 'aunts'. This had not applied to him; he was never an uncle. The name Romany extended from 1931 until his death in 1943. Muriel and Doris, two young ladies who featured in the radio rambles, were fond of recalling when Romany entered the studio in Manchester to record an instalment of his series, wearing his parson's garb. At another time he might be clad in some favourite old clothes.

Romany drove a car, which enabled him to discover the beauties of dales and wind-swept moorland. In books and radio programmes a horse-drawn caravan known as 'the vardo' was his picturesque transport. Being a base for his nature studies, they gave him some excellent sermon material.

On his visits to Old Parks Farm, Romany lost no time in striding through the orchard and down a steep, grassy bank to the beck, which was overhung with alders and willows. He would cross the beck by the trunk of a fallen tree and hoped to arrive on the other side with dry feet. Romany looked for curlew nests in the meadows and buzzard nests on the old oak trees. He would sit and behold the Lakeland hills. I visited his main haunts when the Lakeland fell known as Saddleback was a deep blue against a sky that was uniformly grey with cloud.

G. Bramwell Evans, also known as 'Romany'.

Travellers in Lunesdale.

Chatting with a lile porter at the nearest station on the Settle-Carlisle railway, I discovered that when this railwayman started work, in a minor capacity, the stationmaster had mentioned that there would be a parcel on the next train that had to be treated with great respect. Inside what looked like an ordinary parcel were the ashes of Romany. They were to be scattered on a hillock at Old Parks Farm, where a memorial to his great life was created.

Charlie Emmett, an old friend of mine, regarded Romany as 'an ideal I longed to emulate. He was a man of great understanding; and, sadly, when he died, there was no one to fill his shoes'. Romany's death was during the Second World War. His place in the BBC Children's Hour was taken by Norman Ellison, who became widely known as Nomad the Naturalist.

Donald Campbell, High Speed on Water

When I visited the village of Coniston, three names usually flashed through my mind— Sir Malcolm Campbell, his son Donald Campbell CBE and a speedboat known as *Bluebird*. Between them they set no less than eleven speed records on water and ten on land. Donald's restlessness came about from his desire to pass the achievements of his father. Malcolm had been the first person to install a jet engine into a high-speed water craft. His son Donald died, alas, while traversing a stretch of Coniston Water in a boat named *Bluebird*. Donald had broken world speed records in the 1950 and '60s. His sad demise occurred when he faced another attempt on the fourth day of January in 1967.

Donald used a slipway that was associated with his father. The weather in mid-December proved chancy. When climatic conditions settled down on Christmas Day, Donald gathered a scratch team and decided to have two runs in *Bluebird*, looking to achieve speeds in the region of 280 miles per hour. They were not official figures; no time-keepers were present. The best figure at around this time topped the 300 mph mark. *Bluebird* was powered by a jet engine that, hopefully, would enable Donald to improve on his world water speed record of 276.33 mph. The first run saw the *Bluebird* attain a speed of 297 mph. Donald, for his record attempt, took the *Bluebird* into deep water. Buoys marked the measured kilometre. Speed was increased. The jet engine screamed. *Bluebird* lifted and streaked, southwards. Alas, as she came within 100 yards of the second and last kilometre marker, she soared vertically some 50 feet into the air, flipped over on her back and crashed, sinking in water that was 125 feet deep. The wreckage of the boat was not recovered until October 2000. When the body of Donald was brought out of Coniston Water on 28 May 2001, it was still adorned by blue nylon overalls. The grave of this brave man can be seen in the local cemetery.

Lady Anne Clifford,
Last of Her Line

Well over half a century has passed since I was ushered into the Great Hall of Appleby Castle by Lord Hothfield. In a brief chat, he told me about his family association with the county town of Westmorland. We stood before The Great Picture that was commissioned by an ancestor, Lady Anne Clifford; it commemorated her inheritance of the family estate. The picture, which takes the form of a triptych (having three panels), showed Lady Anne at various stages of her life. A painting of an ageing Lady Anne held my attention—she looked sternly down on his Lordship and myself. He was the first to speak, remarking, 'She was quite a gal.' Here was a woman who fought by all means short of outright violence for her rights and who eventually inherited Clifford territory, including much land in old-time Westmorland.

She was born in Skipton. So was I. My favourite walk was 'up the Bailey', beside the high, grey wall of the Castle grounds. I heard so many tales about Lady Anne that I began to think of her as a member of the family—an aunt, perhaps. Lady Anne had been raised in the south, where she was twice married and had five children. Her northern connection did not begin until she approached the age of sixty. Caring for her lands and properties kept her bright-eyed and alert for a further twenty-six years.

Lady Anne was akin to a Queen in Westmorland, her spirit enduring at Pendragon, Brough, Appleby and Brougham. For over three centuries, the Cliffords dominated the county of Westmorland. She was the most prominent of the Cliffords in the Eden Valley context, the last of her line. Her full title included Countess Dowager of Pembroke, Dorset and Montgomery.

Lady Anne restored Pendragon Castle, which—having a history that went back to the twelfth century—had been knocked about by the Scots. A farmer I met at a local auction mart had chanted, 'Let Uther Pendragon do what he can; Eden shall run as Eden ran.' This refers to a tradition that the mythical father of King Arthur built the original Pendragon. The structure was not old enough for that and it was said that Uther's plan to make the river surround the castle would not work. The water would not oblige.

Martin Holmes, of Appleby, who outlined the life of Lady Anne in *Proud Northern Lady*, referred to a popular image of Anne as an autocrat and terrifying old person who had a caustic tongue. He concluded that this was unmerited. Lady Anne—twice (unhappily) married, twice widowed—was proud of her status and of her family. Among her honourable titles was that of Sheriff of Westmorland. The Civil War made a visit to her northern inheritance unsafe. Then, in the summer of 1649, when she had attained the age of fifty-nine, she travelled northwards on a tour of inspection. This post-Civil War spree was completed fifteen years later.

Lady Anne was passionately fond of castles. She also had a deep love for churches, some of which she restored. In fact she restored many old buildings At Appleby, her name and the date, 1655, were carved on a rafter of the Lady Chapel in the south aisle to mark her repair. She founded the hospital of St Anne for twelve poor women and, at Beamsley, completed work on her mother's hospital. Other restoration work was put in hand. Marie Hartley, a dale-country historian I had known for some years, believed that this building programme—'as we might call it now'—cost Lady Anne £40,000. The money would be legitimately drawn from the rents of her estates.

Her Ladyship gloried when travelling by horse-drawn coach on roads where this form of transport had been previously unknown. No less than six horses were harnessed to her coach and she was accompanied, on board, by her 'two gentlewomen and [her] woman servants'. Menservants were on horseback.

She was generous to the needy, making gifts to friends and (on special occasions) handing over a copy of a favourite portrait. She died in 1676 at the age of eighty-six. There was a grand funeral at St Lawrence's Church at Appleby. Her coffin, made of lead, was fitted with handles so that it might be carried down a flight of eight steps into a vault of modest size. Her body lies mouldering in a tomb, but her spirit goes marching on. Dr G. C. Williamson, who wrote a book about Lady Anne, made what he considered to be a fair estimate of her character:

Taking into consideration the position to which she was born, and viewing her against the background of the times, I cannot but feel that both the seventeenth century and posterity would have been the poorer without her.

W. G. Collingwood, Links with Ruskin

At the Ruskin Museum at Coniston I came face to face with a model of W. G. Collingwood. This notable writer, artist and antiquary was a one-time secretary to Ruskin, one of the most eminent Victorians. Ruskin had spent the latter part of his life at Brantwood, on the shores of Coniston Water. Having a splendid view of the Old Man and a retinue of lofty hills, Ruskin wrote: 'Mountains are the beginning and the end of all natural scenery.'

Collingwood, handsome and moustached, was a Lakelander by adoption. He was born in Liverpool in 1864. His father was a landscape painter. As a youngster, Collingwood accompanied dad on sketching tours. He studied philosophy and aesthetics at University College Oxford, and in 1872 became acquainted, as secretary and literary assistant, with the illustrious John Ruskin, who had moved into Brantwood, on the posh side of Coniston Water. It would be Ruskin's last home. Collingwood (often referred to simply as 'WG') married Edith Isaac, the daughter of a corn merchant, in Maldon, Essex. Travelling to the Lake District, they had resided at Gillhead for nine years before moving to Lanehead, a mile north of Brantwood.

Ruskin came into his story. He was fond of touring the alpine areas of Europe. His visits to Lakeland and Scotland began in 1824; in 1837 he attained a milestone in his busy and highly educational life when, at the age of eighteen, he had a second tour of the Lake District. That summer he was contrasting the cottages of Italy with those he had experienced in Westmorland. The Collingwoods were neither posh nor especially affluent. They had an enjoyable view of the lake, on which they found pleasure in sailing; also in view was a grand array of fell. In Brantwood, WG edited the *Transactions* of the Cumberland and Westmorland Antiquarian Society, jotting down memories and impressions of Lakeland life. *Coniston Water, Past and Present*, which appeared in 1902, contains a reference by Collingwood to old-time industries, noting:

> Along the beach and in every little dell where an unfailing streamlet runs down, there used to be iron furnaces [bloomeries] where small charges of ore, brought on pack-horses and boats from Low Furness, were smelted with charcoal.

At this time the woods were being felled and nearly destroyed. Collingwood recalled:

> [A time] when the barren hills were only varied by smoking 'pitsteads', where charcoal was made, and flaming 'hearths' where grimy workers toiled at the bellows, or shovelled

the red ore and black coals, with shouts and rattling, and the thud of the little water-wheels that worked the hammers and drove the blast…

Coniston became a touristy village in Collingwood's time. In 1897 he was at John Ruskin's beck and call—if Ruskin had a bright idea, it was usually Collingwood who carried it out. After Ruskin's death, Collingwood planned a memorial exhibition at Coniston and established the Ruskin Museum in the village. When he had a trip to Iceland, Collingwood returned to the Lake District with a tanned and neatly bearded face. During the homeward voyage he was mistaken as the ship's captain!

For the 1897 visit to Iceland he was in the company of Dr John Stefannson, an Icelandic scholar. They travelled mainly in the south and west, recording their journey in book form. Entitled *A Pilgrimage to the Saga-steads of Iceland*, it was published in 1899. I saw a copy of the work at the home of friends living near Reykjavik. The imprint indicated that the work had been published by W. Holmes, Lightburne Road, Ulverston.

Collingwood, a stylish writer, penned *Thurston on the Mere,* dealing with Norse times in the Coniston area. His book *The Lake Counties*, published in 1931, was applauded by Sir Hugh Walpole, who observed in *The Times* that a friend had described it as the finest guide book in English, and a book that contained 'the grandest prose-writing about the Lake District in existence'. Collingwood had a light touch; his work was never stilted. He showed just as much interest in people as in places. He designed the Ruskin memorial cross in the churchyard at Coniston, and on his death, on 20 January 1900, he was buried in that yard, the grave being adorned by a tall greenstone cross. A small self-portrait of Collingwood is to be seen in Brantwood. There are, of course, larger studies of Ruskin.

Peter Delap,
Doctor and Deerologist

My friendship with Dr Peter Delap sprang from a mutual love of wild deer. I first met him as a fellow committee member at Hay Bridge, the astonishing little nature reserve in the Duddon Valley. Our exchange of letters began in the autumn of 1967. A passion for deer, mainly red and roe, kept Peter sane in his stressful job as medical practitioner in the market town of Appleby. He would take me up to the attic of his large white-painted house. I saw rows of antlers arranged on the wooden floor.

Peter watched his red deer on and around Martindale, to the west of Ullswater. The roe inhabited some of the local woods. It amused me that he should be so lightly clad when venturing on to the Lakeland fells, which he sometimes did in fading light after a busy surgery. He was inconspicuous by intent, wearing drab clothes and a floppy hat; he donned sandals, not boots. He was a prime supporter of nature conservation during what he called 'a long and lucky life', born into a family of Scottish origins who made Ireland their home in the reign of Elizabeth I. He was one of the members of the Mammal Society. It became the nucleus of the British Deer Society, which based its logo on the head of a Winster stag that had been collected by Peter and was displayed outdoors at his home.

Out-of-doors, little escaped his attention. In the summer of 1975, in a letter he sent to me, he reported having found the site on the Lakeland fells where an American fighter plane had crashed. A crater worthy of a 500-lb bomb, with myriad shards, had scattered over a full acre. The only beneficiary was the rare cloudberry, now sprouting green and fresh through heather and sedge blotted brown by the explosion.

Peter wrote to me amusingly of the situation at the north end of Claife Heights, west of Windermere Lake. In 1970, nineteen red hinds were eating their way down off the hill-top every night, to be met at dawn by forty feral grey geese dining on their way up from Esthwaite. In between was a thin straddle of starving sheep. It was at Claife that Peter made a special study of a red stag he called Old Crabbie, so named because of the shape of its top tines, which Peter fancied were like a crab's pincer. He kept his eye on Crabbie for six years and collected an impressive number of its cast antlers.

On a late August day in 1976, Peter had an enjoyable time showing off local deer to a doctor and his seventeen-year-old son from Exmoor. Keen deerologists, they were left impressed yet shattered! Starting from the head of Haweswater they first met a score of absurdly tame Canada geese, plus one Greylag, at the mouth of Riggindale Beck. Their progression took them up to the rim of Welter Crag with a nice breeze at 2,000 feet. It was a good stalk, during which they photographed deer hinds and calves. Then it was over High Street to the cliffs of the topmost Martindale corrie. Peter and his friends were thankful to find sixty-five stags were congregated here. 'The only royal and a nice ten-pointer were just beginning to clear velvet.'

When I took up sika deer-watching in Bowland, little was known about the field characteristics of this species in England. Correspondence with Peter Delap revived in him memories of watching sika in his old Powerscort days in Ireland. I sent him copies of my copious field notes and invariably had informative replies. His research helped me considerably and it was with great sadness that I heard of his death on 1 November 2002 at the age of eighty-nine. Some years later I wrote a short book about his remarkable life entitled *Peter Delap: Doctor and Deerologist*.

A local man in Martindale, known to the author, with a hand-reared red deer stag.

Edward Elgar,
His Lakes Overture

'Not a word could be got out of him, and then, suddenly, he began to write furiously.' In these words did Dr Charles William Buck, of Giggleswick, describe the response of Edward Elgar to his first sight of Windermere. The two young men had met at a soiree organised when members of the British Medical Association gathered in Worcester in 1882. Elgar raised an orchestra for that soiree. Buck was persuaded to take his cello and play it with others when the final conference took place.

Elgar and Buck found pleasure in talk about music, in animals (especially dogs), and in country life. Buck invited his new friend to visit his home (and surgery) overlooking the Market Place at Settle in North Ribblesdale. Later, the good doctor and his family occupied a venerable house at the lower end of Belle Hill, in adjacent Giggleswick. The two men chatted on musical matters as they bestrode the limestone hills. Occasionally, they were seated in the good doctor's horse-drawn trap as he undertook his medical rounds. Elgar spent some time with some of Buck's friends in his music room.

Elgar wrote to Buck in 1899 about some good old days:

> A patch in the old year which bears thinking of with pleasure was our little visit to Settle—it was very gratifying to take my wife amongst the old scenes and to find us welcomed and my miserable self not quite forgotten.

They also grew to love the Lake District. In clear weather Elgar, standing on the grey rim of Giggleswick Scar, would see the imposing fells of Lakeland straddling the north-western skyline.

Buck took his friend to the Lake District. They beheld Windermere, the viewpoint Elgar visiting being possibly Orrest Head. How did the two friends travel from Giggleswick to Windermere? Presumably by rail, changing at Lancaster, disembarking from the Lancaster-Carlisle line at Oxenholme and taking a train that clattered and tooted its way to the terminal at what had been the hamlet of Birthwaite—changed to Windermere, after the name of the adjacent lake.

Elgar, visiting the Lake District several times, developed a love for the area of lakes and fells. He was so moved that he composed a 'Lakes Overture'. It had been referred to by Buck in conversation and by Elgar in one of the many letters he wrote to his friend over a spell of half a century. The musical score has not been seen or heard since 8 March 1885,

Edward Elgar, 1899.
(*Elliott and Fry*)

when Elgar informed Buck that 'the lakes overture is done with—I am on the Scotish [*sic.*] lay just now & have a big work in tow.'

Elgar's mysterious overture was in my mind as I climbed Orrest Head for a grand view of Windermere, the lake that had stirred Elgar's imagination. On a visit to Lakeland in 1911, he entrained for Penrith and travelled by horse-drawn coach to Ullswater and Patterdale, staying at the *White Lion*. In the following year he was accompanied by Alice, his wife. They crossed Kirkstone Pass to Ambleside and Grasmere, where he booked accommodation for them at the *Prince of Wales* hotel. Elgar and two ladies—his wife and one of her friends—visited Wastwater, admiring the fan-shaped screes above the lake and the pyramidic form of Great Gable at the dalehead. On other days, they visited monastic remains—the ruins of Calder Abbey and those of Furness Abbey in the Vale of the Deadly Nightshade.

The outbreak of war in 1914 had a shattering effect on the composer. German audiences had responded warmly to his musical efforts when he had visited that land. Richter had, indeed, championed his music in England. The Elgars did manage a wartime visit to the Ullswater area in 1916, spending a few days in the company of the daughter of Edward Speyer. Alice Elgar described a voyage on the lake as 'very nice', though when a storm arrived she and Elgar had to snuggle in the lee of an umbrella. Rain was falling with tropical intensity. A man, who had been standing by, talking with another, suddenly put his face close to theirs and said, 'You are lovers still—like me and my wife.' Elgar sweetly remarked, 'I hope so.' Alice concluded her note with the words: 'It was quite sincere and very touching.'

The most memorable Elgar connection for me came when I visited a farmhouse in the southern part of Lakeland. During the Second World War, Buck's daughter Monica and her husband, beset by bombing, moved from their London home to the sanctuary of a farmhouse in the Lake District. They were later permitted by the farmer to create an extension to the farmhouse. My dear wife, Freda, and I visited some time after the Londoners had died. A grandfather clock stood in isolation. It had a rather bland appearance—the clock face had been removed, the space being covered by pieces of polished oak. With permission, I opened the door of the tall clock and released a cascade of printed music, among which was a batch of hand-written compositions signed by Edward Elgar and dated back to the 1880s. This music had been composed at what Elgar playfully called Giggleswyke.

Having been kindly given the scores by the farmer's wife, I published them in booklet form, distributing them free of charge. The original scores were donated to the Elgar Birthplace Museum at Broadheath in 1990. They were received by Wulstan Atkins, godson of Elgar, who remarked, 'It's wonderful to see these remarkable early Elgar scores after all these years. We are deeply grateful they have come to the birthplace, where they will be well looked after.' Before handing them over, I dined with Wulstan and Christopher Harmer, vice-chairman of the Elgar Foundation.

I did not succeed in tracking down the score of 'Lakes Overture'. Elgar had some Scottish music in mind at the time and might have absorbed a dash of Lakeland in a piece relating to water on land north of the Scottish border.

During another visit to this Lakeland farmhouse, my wife occupied an unusual but attractive chair made of polished wood. Attached to it was a wooden tray which could be either swung to allow someone to sit down or, indeed, to hold music in repose. The chair had been a gift to Dr Buck from Elgar, who must have composed music while sitting there. It was named 'Elgar's Chair'. I like to think that occasionally it had provided a ledge on which Elgar could jot down some of his compositions.

Elgar did not forget the grandeur of Lakeland, which was so different from the rounded hills, the woods and orchards of his native Worcestershire.

12

Tissie Fooks,
Life in the Rusland Valley

When Herbert and Helen Fooks first saw a big barn at Hay Bridge, in the Rusland Valley, they felt to be on a tour of exploration. The local estate, with two farmsteads, had just come on the market. The picture of Herbert below is taken from a display at Hay Bridge. Helen—known to her friends as Tissie—recalled for me a winter day in 1957. As they approached the area from a lane that began in the village of Bouth, a mile away, they had almost to fight their way through a tangle of bracken and trees. It was impossible to use a car or even a Land Rover.

Bob Longmire, who lived in the village, cut a broad swathe through the bracken. Tissie recalled:

> It was late afternoon when we found the barn. We had a sort of telescopic view— through the gaps where the doors had been—of distant snow-covered hills, on which lay a pink light. I thought: 'What a place for a house!' I made my husband promise faithfully that if we bought the estate we would convert the barn into a house.

The barn, blocking out half the sky, would have needed the expenditure of over £1,000 for safe-guarding. It was promptly demolished.

They moved into Low Hay Bridge in 1958. Her son John drew the plans for the modification of High Hay Bridge into a house. It retained its local character—a large piece of Lakeland slate became the mantelpiece, and slate from Broughton became the sills for the kitchen windows and the working surfaces. I got to know it well. Basically, there were two large openings. One was to admit old-time laden hay carts, while the other, a facing door, had been used to toss hay to cattle in the stalls below. The walls and high-beamed ceilings were left as they were. After allowing for an air cavity, an inner 'skin' of thermalite blocks was added. I have a special memory of the wood-burning fireplace, which, some 6 feet wide, was set at one end. At meetings and on private occasions when I reclined here, chattering, I was stared at by the mounted head of a moose. It had been affixed to an enormous chimney breast. This had been painted white to reflect light from the expansive windows.

In the main room, walls were lined by coarse fabric so that Herbert might display many of his sporting trophies. Another barn on the estate was re-roofed and re-floored, becoming a deer museum. Herbert Fooks was a sporty type; he had arrived in Lakeland

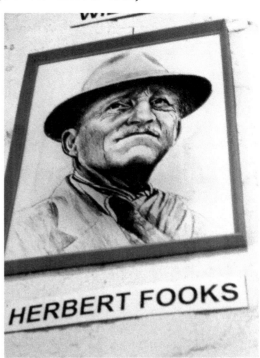

HERBERT FOOKS

Herbert Fooks, a pioneer in wildlife
education in the Lake District.

as the Forestry Commission's first game warden. At Low Hay Bridge, the age of the
farmhouse was deduced on the discovery of a record that a child was baptised from here
in 1615.

High Hay Bridge was a home with a magnificent view. I would look northwards over
a paddock with deer and a pond adorned by waterfowl. Josephine, a roe doe, was the
oldest inhabitant, occupying a large enclosure to be viewed from the back of the house.
When I last knew her she was nine years of age. Helen mentioned that the deer had been
born on the main road near Windermere, her mother having been chased off by dogs.
In view, in another direction, were some stately fells, including Coniston Old Man and
Wetherlam (looking shyly over Bethecar).

It was a joy to motor from Bouth to the reserve through a well-wooded countryside
with lots of deer—red and roe in the woods and also in some of the enclosures. When I
attended committee meetings in the home I would keep glancing out of the window at
the bountiful wildlife, birds and beasts. There was a dovecote—but few live doves. A pair
of sparrow-hawks had settled in the district. I saw one of them pluck a dove from the sky.

Charcoal-burning had taken place in local woods and was recalled when a conical hut,
of the type used by burners of the past was erected at Hay Bridge. Life for the charcoal
burner and his family was no sinecure. The work being invariably carried out in the
forest, groups of charcoal burners, moving from one area to another, lived a nomadic
existence in the hand-made type of hut built from a skeleton of wooden poles covered

The main room of High Hay Bridge.

with turf and sacking. If timber was plentiful and an enduring stay became likely, a wooden floor might be laid. Separate huts accommodated beds of brushwood and straw-filled sacks. A metal drum, lagged with turf, provided cooking facilities. Trees were not uprooted; they were felled to within a foot of the ground. Within fifteen years new shoots had sprouted from the stool. The mixed woodlands were maintained.

When I last saw Tissie I was breaking a journey from Lakeland to my home. It was a chilling autumn day. I shared the approach road with one or two roe deer. In the big house Tissie was in the kitchen. Smiling broadly, she handed me a mug of hot tea. We recalled the days when Dr Peter Delap, of Appleby, who joyfully watched red deer, was a regular visitor. He would sometimes spend a night in a wooden hut standing just off the lane leading to the house.

After Tissie died a memorial was raised to her. Stand hereabouts and you can view the reserve and, on the horizon, a range of Lakeland hills. There might even be a feral deer in view. The Rusland Valley is such a favourite of mine that I later named my house 'Rusland' in its honour.

13

Bill Grant, Forest and Theatre

The roaring of Furness red deer stags was clearly heard in October by Bill Grant and his wife, Elsie, as they entered or departed from *Deer Close*, their bungalow, situated in Grizedale Forest. It was close to but much higher than the grey surface of Coniston Water. October was mating time for the red deer; they were rutting.

Grizedale was a mixed forest with a belt of hardwoods along the sides of the Grizedale valley. When I first knew the forest there were nearly 1,000 acres of old-style sessile oak woodland. The springtime colours, as the leaves unfolded, were almost as attractive as those of autumn. With the Japanese larch you got attractive red twigs in a setting of light-green needles.

Bill, chief forester at Grizedale, regularly saw an old stag, black and dripping from wallowing in a peaty pool, and on its rounds, cross the front of the house. His wife, looking from one of the rear windows of their home, viewed red deer. A party of hinds was confiding. They had occasionally to be vocally admonished.

In 1972, I decided to spend some time listening to the vocal stags. Bill had become an old friend of mine through membership of the local branch of the British Deer Society. He had an especially busy life. It was at Grizedale, two years before, that the capercaillie was reintroduced into England as a nesting species. During one of my forest walks, seeking deer, I was eyed by a cock capercaillie the size of a small turkey; it roosted in a tree.

Bill helped with the reintroduction of the greylag goose into England as a nesting species. Ere long, greylags were nesting on the shores of the lake, though not always successfully because of innumerable visitors. Bill had set up boxes in which the smaller species of bird might nest.

He was founder and director in 1986 of what became known as the Theatre in the Forest. The idea had come to Bill when he visited America on a Winston Churchill Fellowship, intent on studying wildlife conservation, with special emphasis on the educational aspects. Bill went up to London with £800 in his pocket, having been instructed by his committee to spend it on a piano—the best obtainable. It was purchased in 1971. The Theatre was in the upper room of a Stable Block that had been associated with Grizedale Hall, which the Brocklebank family—wealthy ship-owners—had built in the first decade of the century. The Grizedale estate came to the Forestry Commission when it was offered to the government in lieu of death duties. During the Second World

Red stags at rutting time in Lowther Park.

War the Hall had been a prisoner of war camp for German aviators and submariners. It was demolished in 1957.

The Theatre, which I occasionally attended, was in space that had been used for hay and other types of fodder. It became an auditorium 80 feet long and some 35 feet wide. Another section, converted into a bar-foyer, had a length of 40 feet and the same width as the auditorium. The only contractor who worked on the scheme of converting it into a smart theatre was an electrician; the rest was by voluntary labour. Visitors to the Theatre in the Forest usually arrived at the most enchanting time—just before dark. The forest setting, with its varied wildlife, added greatly to the pleasure of a visit.

Bill Grant, Head
Forester at
Grisedale Forest.

Leslie Grisedale, Shap Fell

Both Leslie and his wife came from families that had been Lakeland farmers for generations. I first met Leslie in 1953. For six years he had lived and worked well on Shap Fell, over 1,000 feet above sea level. The next habitation to his was half a mile away. His charges—well over 500 sheep—roamed across 550 windswept acres. Most of Leslie's recollections were about winter conditions on the fells. On 29 January 1947, the fell country had been 'wrapped up' in snow since Christmas. Sam Barnett, of Shap Lodge, had the care of almost 2,000 sheep on the fell. Leslie observed, 'We never saw a blade of grass for eight weeks ... It was well into March before the hill-ends were visible once again.' When lambing time began there was still plenty of snow on the high and rough acres. After snow came frost!

Leslie had an anxious time one day when he was swept down a fell in an avalanche. He had been walking round the crag ends when the snow broke. Happily, most of the fall was before him rather than at his back, which could have been disastrous. He recalled, 'The dogs were with me. We were carried down to within 500 yards of the main road.' Looking after sheep was not the only farm task to occupy his mind. He was also concerned with the maintenance of stone walls made without as much as a dab of mortar.

Supplies of coal were delivered to Leslie's home. There was also reliance on peat to take the chill out of the air of some of the rooms. The peat was cut and stacked just before lambing time. Three or four weeks later, the peat turves were turned. They could then be thoroughly dried by wind and sun. Peat was stacked on the fell just before haytime, being brought down to the house as required. Leslie liked a peat fire, remarking that a lot of people objected to the white dust that peat left everywhere in a room. 'There was always a bit of dirt in a farmhouse. And this peat was clean dirt after all!'

Eric Halsall,
One Man and His Dog

It was Eric Halsall, a quietly-spoken man from Lancashire, who was the commentator when the BBC televised sheepdog trials, many of them being held in Lakeland. Each programme had the unforgettable title of *One Man and His Dog*. I met Eric in the spring of 1990 at his home, a trim bungalow at Cliviger, which stands not far from Burnley. The subject of our conversation quickly sped from Lancashire to old-time Lakeland. The appeal of Lakeland began in his Boy Scout days, when he did a lot of walking in the district. He told me that 'many a time, after arriving on a late train at Windermere station, have I tramped down the side of Lake Windermere at dead of night to reach the Great Tower site—"a great Scout area"—on Cartmel Fell.' He added, 'You can't beat the fells and mountains.'

At a time in Eric's memory a Lakeland hill man was expected to pay about £5 for an unbroken collie dog. The BBC had completed a fourteen-episode series of *One Man and His Dog* in Derbyshire, but the first programme had been 'shot' at Buttermere in 1975—which, said Eric, gave the general public a glimpse of one of the most attractive parts of Lakeland 'and a view of sheepdogs they had never seen before.' The spectators responded quickly to the quality of the scenery, the aptitude of the collies and the tense competition that occurred between men who, otherwise, were good friends.

The Buttermere experiment came off, though it had tense moments. In the following year, the team was back in Lakeland, gathering at a farm by Loweswater. The fourth series was filmed in Rannerdale, by the side of Crummock Water, and the tenth by Ullswater. Beatrix Potter countryside provided a lovely backdrop for the thirteenth, which was 'shot' in 1988.

Seven cameras were used. Thick and heavy cables extended across country—yet no observer of a sheepdog trial was aware of them. Herdwicks, the little sheep of Lakeland, had been used for the 'practice' runs—to site the cameras—but not for filming. The preference was for sheep of the Swaledale type. Herdwicks, living on herby ground among rocks on the fells, were too individualistic to permit themselves to be pushed around at speed.

Eric developed a great fondness for the Lakes and had lots of Lakeland farming friends. He judged many sheepdog trials, including the celebrated 'dog day' at Rydal. In 1988 he judged in Patterdale. Said he, 'My Lakeland friends really know the value of a good working collie to help manage their flocks.'

Once, when I left Eric, I followed a moorland road and came up against a flock of sheep being driven. Men and dogs did their best to keep the sheep moving in good order. One Lakeland motorist who found himself in similar circumstances became desperate, remarking to the nearest farmer, 'Who is the master of this flock?' The man replied, 'That little black-faced begger at t'front.'

Joseph Hardman,
Prime Photographer

Lakeland folk, set against a background of lakes and fells, have been recorded in various ways, not least through photography. Among the pioneer photographers in the district was George Percy Abraham, born in London in 1846 and trained by Elliot and Fry. He had travelled to Keswick to help Alfred Pettit for a season. Liking what he saw, and with the help of Mark Shearman, he established a small, wooden photography shop at the corner of Lake Road. He married Mary Dixon, a local lass, and they had two sons, George and Ashley, who followed on in the family business. Abraham photographs became notable, many of them portraying climbers in courageous rock-climbing feats.

Cameras were still a novelty when Henry Herbert arrived in Bowness to work for Brunskills, who, in the 1880s, were well-established as photographers. The Herbert family had invested in a small cart to transport the equipment. A 'dark-room' consisted of a small tent set on a tripod; the base of the tent could be tied around the photographer's waist to ensure that his work area was light-proof. Admitted light, filtered through a small red window, did not affect the plates.

When I edited the magazine *Cumbria*, Joseph Hardman of Kendal was a photographer who sent me lots of prints. He had carried the tradition of plate cameras into the modern age. Joseph, born at Radcliffe, near Manchester, in 1897, began his working life at the age of eleven. He became a 'half-timer' at a factory producing shuttles for the cotton mills. Taking up a menial job at Kendal, he joined a local photographic society, acquired a plate-camera and, when I chatted with him in 1953, had an accumulated stock of almost 50,000 negatives.

Joseph, heavily-built and fresh-faced, was happy to be out and about in the Lake District most days of the week. He captured, through the medium of photography, the ever-changing moods of the countryside, travelling about the Lake District in a car driven by a friend or in a hired taxi. He sometimes covered 200 miles a day. Said Joseph, 'I think I do better when I'm in the back of a car … I don't miss much then!' He and his wife worked as a perfect team.

His photography was never flat, taken with the sun tanning the back of his neck. Crags or trees, animals or people were used to create striking patterns. Glance at one of his monochrome prints and you might tell the time of the day and the season of the year in which it had been taken. Many of his photographs relating to Lakeland farming were taken before the time of radical change—horses being replaced by tractors. Joseph was at his best when the lens of his camera was facing the broad sweep of a Lakeland hill or the shimmering waters of a lake. His wife was a devoted assistant. He would fix his heavy camera on to a substantial tripod and she attended to the plates, receiving those that had been exposed and handing him others which were prepared for exposure. The weight must have been considerable.

Joseph Hardman sometimes added glamour to his Lakeland scenic shots by taking along nurses from the Kendal hospital. In return for their 'days out' they posed—demurely, of course—in various places, such as at the Surprise View above Derwentwater. Each August, a batch of photographs from 'J. Hardman' contained snow pictures with young ladies holding sprigs of holly.

Much of his work is preserved in the archives of Abbot Hall, Kendal. He was not discouraged if the shadows lengthened and the light began to fade; for Joseph, there was always that odd shaft of sunlight to bring out a subject against a dark background. He often worked close to the edge of darkness.

Cumbria magazine received lots of his photos by post and I met him now and again. He spent a good deal of time setting up his large camera on a substantial tripod, draping cloth over his head as he peered through his camera lens to reassure himself that the image was satisfactory. We sometimes met in the Lyth Valley at blossom time. He photographed Shepherds' Meets when they were held at the old *Dun Bull* inn, before Haweswater was converted into a reservoir. He considered that Tarn Hows was the most pictorial part of Lakeland.

Some of his best character studies were of Isaac Cookson, of Helton, who had attended Mardale Meets for sixty-one years. Among the photographs he sent to me in a card-backed envelope was a study of a large flock of sheep that, having wintered on the Cartmel Fells, were being driven home to Hawes, in Wensleydale—a distance of over 40 miles. The work was being done to a strict timetable. Joseph had positioned himself in the main street of Kendal on the appointed day. He wanted to have the imposing Town Hall in the background.

Joseph and his wife usually relaxed, holiday-wise, at Berners Close, Grange-over-Sands, or at Blackpool. He died in 1972, but his photographic work will never be forgotten.

Haweswater.

17

W. Heaton Cooper, Artist and Climber

Hanging above my fireplace is the reproduction of a painting by W. Heaton Cooper—a study, at eventide, of Wastwater, Great Gable and attendant fells. It was a gift from my three fellow Geriatric Blunderers who had accompanied me through the list of 214 Wainwrights, the peaks featured by the man who inspired many a walker through his unique books. A note on the back extended good wishes to me for climbing so many fells—and to my wife for letting me!

W. Heaton Cooper, who combined art with climbing, was reared at what would become known as Gatehouse at Coniston. His father, Alfred Heaton Cooper, born in 1863, was the son of a bookkeeper in a Bolton cotton mill. His mother had come from Norway. He spent several years in his father's studio, jibbed at a career in accountancy at the Town Hall and gained a scholarship to Westminster School of Art in London.

Alfred was at his best when portraying the interplay of natural scenes at specific times of day and season. He was also fascinated to see native Lakelanders at work in various rural settings. He gave his son his first lesson in painting and first directed his thoughts to the natural splendour, colour and form of the district. A few years at the Royal Academy School added valuable experience to the young painter's career. The artwork of W. Heaton Cooper is memorable. I met him at Winterseeds, to which he, his wife, Ophelia Gordon Bell, and their young family had moved in 1949. The front windows framed a view of Grasmere Vale. He implied that the name Winterseeds is Norse, relating to a high, windy, dairy farm. The buildings of the Norse period would have been in wood, on the foundations of which the stone building would have been grafted.

Like much of the artist's work, the treatment of the aforementioned Wasdale subject is delicate and subtle. If I flop into a chair after a busy spell, such a large picture is a balm to my riven spirits. I feel I can look right into the view, with its shadowy boulders and the double-beauty of Gable and his reflection in the lake. All the features are bonded by geology, by delicate hues, by the special aura of mountain country—and, in this case, by a dash of spirituality.

Art and climbing became genuine passions for Heaton Cooper. He kept a large studio in Grasmere and 'did rock-climbing for fun'. When I asked him what the average climber was wearing in the 1920s, he replied, 'I did not know any average climbers. I knew what I wore, which was ordinary tweeds and sweater—usually two sweaters.' On an expedition

W. Heaton Cooper.

to the fells he carried a bag of raisins and sugar, taking a mouthful now and again when he felt hungry. 'Sometimes I took sandwiches, sometimes an onion. I got the idea of eating an onion from a Lakeland huntsman.'

He did not know any countryside possessing more variety to the square mile as Lakeland. The mountains looked different from whichever side you saw them. The valleys stepped down to the lowlands with the most interesting proportions. Said Heaton Cooper:

> So many things have happened over many millions of years it is no wonder the hills are complex … I like mountain landscape. When I see the bones of the land I realise that mountains are just wrinkles on the face of the earth; that they are rooted in the earth and are part of its skin.

Lakeland colour was very subtle and, on the whole, it was considered to be a country of quiet colours—greys, green, white. He remarked:

> The atmosphere is itself a colour. You get quite a difference between the seasons. Many painters try to make Lakeland too colourful and miss its character. A brightly coloured building can go quite well in Scotland. Here it can't. It looks all wrong. The colour must be quiet.

In his early days as a climber he would cycle to the base of distant crags. Sometimes he might go by bus. 'I very often had to run all the way down from Scafell Pike or Scafell to the Old Dungeon Ghyll to catch the last bus home.' He also went through a motorcycle period, recalling, 'I was so ashamed of the noise the bike made that I soon gave it up.' The first car he got was an Austin 7; it was ten years of age. 'I got it for £6 and, not knowing how to drive it, I taught myself by going out in it.'

Heaton Cooper drawings have been reproduced in many editions of the climbing guides. Photographic illustrations do not reveal a rock structure in sufficient detail for a climber to follow them. A smudge on a photograph might be a juniper bush, a tuft of heather or an overhang. It was fascinating to watch him portraying a leisurely manner at work in his studio.

In his autobiography, he suggested that each subject must be allowed to dictate design and treatment, 'so that every painting becomes a new and exciting adventure'. The sort of mountain country that appealed is where he could look, from a high and broad ridge, containing one or more tarns, to high mountains. An instance of this is the craggy north side of Fairfield from Angle Tarn above Patterdale. The farms and walls were part of the scene because farmers have worked with nature. 'They have put into the land as much as they have taken out. The homesteads seem to have grown, so wonderfully do they fit the land.'

18

Herdwick Men and the Native Sheep

There's a lot of *sad grund* (poor ground) on the fells. The only breed of sheep to be found up here in reasonable numbers was known as the Herdwick. The sheep were 'heafed', which meant that each of them knew its own fell. There was a strong fascination for the tract of land which it had known as a lamb. One afternoon, sitting on a high fell, I glanced at a Herdwick; it had drawn attention to itself by giving me a disdainful sneeze. Here was a member of a wiry, goat-like race, with a deep, round body and rough white face.

There is something almost terrifying about a skull-to-skull collision between two determined tups, remembering that each weighs around a hundredweight and the animals have deliberately charged each other from a distance of several yards. Canon Rawnsley had observed that if any creature knows the misery of headache it will be a Herdwick tup at mating time!

On many occasions during my editorship of *Cumbria* magazine I beheld a member of a race that had been perhaps less influenced by the introduction of outside blood. Thick-boned, sweet-fleshed, the Herdwick is thatched with a fleece that seems more like hair than wool, fit only in man's world for carpets and coarse tweeds but perfectly suited to the climate and conditions on the highest mountains in the land.

James Clarke (1787) was unable to discover where the breed had come from, adding, 'The inhabitants of *Nether Wasdale* say they were taken from on board a stranded ship.' However, until recent times, their number had been very small; 'they grow very little wool; eight or nine of them jointly not producing more than a stone; yet their wool is pretty good.'

The term 'Herdwick' was first used by the Cistercian monks of Furness Abbey. It indicated a sheep farm and was eventually used for the specific breed of sheep. Rawnsley, writing about Herdwicks in 1911, considered them unique in many ways. The word 'Herdwick' suggested to him a warrior breed:

These hardy warriors [*sic.*], it is believed, came over originally to our hills with human warriors of as hardy a make, the Norsemen from over the foam…. By the ruffs of hair upon their necks and the shape of their roman [*sic.*] noses, they were evidently intended to fend of themselves in snowy places where grass was scarce.

It is a joy to see a flock of Herdwick sheep in central Lakeland. The breed, which might have been present in the Bronze Age, was well-distributed in the fell-country of the north-west until the 1920s—then its range began to contract as the Swaledale moved in from the east. However, the Herdwick still holds much of the highest, roughest ground. The breed was at the heart of an old Lakeland economy; it was confined to dales lying at around or a little above sea level, and fells that rose sheer to tickle the clouds at over 2,000 feet. The tenant of a farm accepted a specific number of sheep, selling the wool and any surplus stock. When eventually he gave up the tenancy, he left at the farm the same number of animals in a similar condition to when he had received them. The *heaf*-going instinct was preserved.

Springtime for the Herdwick breed of sheep traditionally began in May, though some of the toughest sheep might have springtime fever a little in advance of this. Most of the Herdwicks and Swaledales that were gathered on the fells were driven to the low country and nibbled their way through fresh greenery of pastures and meadows. When a ewe dropped a lamb, the wee critter would struggle to its feet and shake itself within a short time before questing for mother's teats and nibbling grass. The bleats and baas of sheep in the springtime are constant.

William Wilson, who lived in a house near the outflow of Bassenthwaite Lake, had been known to his friends, over many years, as Herdwick Billy. We conversed about the Herdwick breed, which was in stained glass on a window of the house porch. The two of us had a bad attack of 'spring-fever'. We loved to talk about springtime, during which Nature bestirs herself in an attractive way. It is a time when blackthorn with creamy flowers thrives in the shade of trees. Out on the fells, the fronds of bracken unfurl.

I first met Herdwick Billy in 1958. A stocky man, he wore tweedy clothes, a floppy trilby, a well-used mac and well-polished boots. A moustache of coarse grey hair adorned his face. He had a cheerful expression. He had been born at Wood How Farm, Nether Wasdale—a farm that was being let along with 400 Herdwick sheep. His father kept between 100–200 sheep above this figure. The family moved to Wasdale Head and eventually took charge of three farms. It was mentioned that the Herdwick, a product of local soil and climate, might eat anything green—including holly, ivy and moss from rocks and walls. Said Herdwick Billy, 'They've been bred on these hills. The hardiness in them had mattered.' The only time he had been 'pushed' to fodder Herdwicks was in 1917, when he was living in Watendlath, a lile hamlet tucked out of sight of the world, approached by road from near Keswick. 'It's a real high-lying place. We had a lot of winter that year.'

Herdwick Billy became secretary of the Herdwick Sheep Breeders' Association when the first Flock Book was published in 1920. I joined the Lakeland flockmasters round the pens at Eskdale Show, which had become known as 'Herdwick Royal'. The year was 1963.

It was a delight to hear the old Lakeland form of speech being used. Two farmers were discussing the price of a tup, which was known locally as 'tip':

'Whoo's ta going on today? Hesta any tips to part wid?'
'Well, ev yan or two.'
'This 'esn't mich coat on it.'
'It's reight enuff.'

Right: A Swaledale ewe with twins.

Below: Herdwick sheep at Eskdale Show.

'Whoo mich ista wantin' fer it?'

'Thirty bob.'

'Ah's going to gie thee twenty-five bob.'

'Split it.'

'Reight.'

Eskdale Show, when I knew it, took place at the threshold of another farming year. Farmers gathered for the hiring, for the winter, of Herdwick tups. The tups would be returned to their true-live owners at a get-together in May. That was also a time when monetary settlements were made. A hire charge was, at the time I recall, somewhere between 25s and 30s, though some outstanding tups had been known to cost £40. Outright sale was still exceptional.

A tall, lean farmer who was well-clad and carried an ornate crook pointed out a good example of a Herdwick tup, remarking, 'We like to see a bright-eyed sheep.' That tup was doing its best to break into the next pen!

Joseph Gregg, another Herdwick enthusiast, farmed in Great Langdale. He remarked, 'I left school at the age of thirteen and maybe did more work between nine and thirteen that a lot of folk do in a lifetime.' He was eighty-one years of age when we last chatted; the year was 1974. Joseph served in the Army during the First World War and, when he was demobilised, did a lot of work for Mrs Heelis (Beatrix Potter), who loved Herdwick sheep.

For his first job as shepherd he received as little as £1 (sometimes £1 and 5s) a week, working unnumbered hours in all weathers. He vividly remembered the inter-war slump in trade and remarked that in 1927 a ewe was bringing in a modest £2. Four years later he was not able to sell his ewes for 10s each. 'There were no subsidies then.' The price of stock did not pick up until the next war.

He proudly remarked that he was still working among Herdwick sheep in summer. When he had graded Herdwick tups in 1952, following a good spring and summer, 'thirty of 'em averaged a hundredweight … I've known a hogg [male sheep] weigh 184 lb, though it was brought up as a pet, being run only on the best land and pinching what it could from the farmyard!'

Joseph had heard that a lot of Herdwick wool was made into carpets. A suit made of Herdwick wool was smart but had one fault—'it lasts too long. One year I got eight pounds of wool off a sheep and sent the wool to a firm in the north specialists in making up suits. It was as good as a raincoat.'

A Herdwick sheep will stand a fair amount of bad weather—Joseph added, 'And so does a sheep farmer!' On 27 March 1919 he was drystone walling—helping to patch up some gaps:

We had to carry stones a long way up the fell before we could start work. We decided to have dinner—and sat down to enjoy our packed meals. There wasn't a cloud in the sky. You couldn't have had a finer March day—but t'sheep started moving down. They were all bleating. It was a sign that a storm was not far away.

By the time the men had finished dinner it was snowing, out of a blue sky it seemed:

> Before we got home it had put down 6 or 7 inches of snow and was blowing it. We'd not been long at home when we had to turn out with a dog, one that was not reputed to do good work but was first-rate at finding sheep. We were pulling sheep out of drifts.

Herbert Grizedale, of Middle Fell, Langdale, told me that five or six times a year men had to go out to rescue sheep that had become cragfast. Herbert had plucked quite a number from Gimmer Crag, Harrison Stickle, Raven Crag and other rock faces. This sort of work was usually undertaken by a team of three men, who used a hempen 'crag rope' that had a length of about 60 feet. Also needed was a finer 'draw rope' with which to lasso a sheep when the man on the main rope was close to the animal.

Stanley Edmondson lived at Seathwaite Farm, at the head of Borrowdale. There were about 80 acres of inside land. I chatted with him in the autumn of 1958, and I was told, 'We're almost in the centre of Lakeland. It's the wettest part of England.' About 120 inches of rain fell on the slates of Seathwaite Farm every year. At nearby Sty Head, the figure was nearer 200. Stanley observed, 'There are many days when the sun shines and the air is dry. Rain comes mainly with the south-westerly winds. It gets away quickly—and it doesn't rain all the time.' Rounding-up the sheep took the Edmondsons about four or five hours. Said Stanley:

> It would be impossible without the help of our five terrier-faced cur dogs. They have tremendous stamina. They give plenty of mouth, which is essential on the fells but is frowned on at sheepdog trials. Up here we need dogs that will rouse the sheep.

Eskdale sheep farmers at the annual show, held at Boot.

It was an Eskdale farmer, with 700 sheep, who furnished me with facts and figures about sheepdogs. The sheep were normally gathered four times a year, a task that took four days. These sheep had extensive pastures on some of the highest peaks in England. Apart from the men, eight dogs did the work of gathering, moving effortlessly about the crags, where, if they had not been disturbed, some sheep would remain hidden—and be missed.

When sheepdogs were ten years old they were getting past their best, though the Eskdale farmer I met had dogs working up to fifteen years of age. No two dogs are quite alike. Some get excited if they are scolded or shouted at—and they do not work properly. There were fast dogs and dogs that took their time. Sheepdogs are gentle with sheep—but rough with foxes. They were known to kill foxes on the fells. There had been no human intervention.

When the Eskdale farmer and his men gathered sheep they went to the highest peaks with a packet of sandwiches for the midday meal. If the sky threatened bad weather they might take a raincoat. They chuckled when they saw holidaymakers staggering along with huge rucksacks on their backs.

19

John Hind,
Tales from Borrowdale

The life of a secluded valley like Borrowdale was richly flavoured by folk tales. When I 'popped in' to see John Hind at Oak Cottage, Ruthwaite, in 1980, he recalled that he had attended the local dale school when there were forty-five names on the register. John left school for work at the age of thirteen; he had been told by the schoolmaster there was nothing more he could do for him so he might as well start work.

It was to be farm work. Over the next few years, John stood at the 'hirings' at Keswick, Cockermouth and Aspatria. Other young hopefuls who gathered at Keswick would be hired for half a year. A hired lad had a week's holiday, joining the farm workers on the following Saturday. John 'lived in' and received a wage of £4 10s for the next six months. Farm work was hard but healthy. Good food was provided for breakfast; there was usually a basin of porridge, bacon sandwich, perhaps a boiled duck egg and scalding tea.

A man who worked in the fields had *bait* (food) delivered to him at 10 in the morning. Typical fare was bread and cheese with a large lump of gingerbread, followed by coffee which was delivered in 'tin bottles'. At ploughing time such a bottle might be hung on a horse's harness until needed. The break at noon for 'dinner' was also an opportunity to feed and rest the horses. The midday meal generally consisted of roast meat with rice pudding or *dumpling* (boiled pudding). Tea was invariably missed out. Supper came at 6 p.m. with a basic ingredient of cold meat.

When John Hind worked at Threlkeld Hall, a farm man, on finishing work for the day, was offered a pint of beer. At haytime it was 'a pint of beer for every cartload of hay delivered after six o'clock'. The scythe in use was usually one of the Yankee-types, with a curved handle. John had mown with one of the old-style, straight-shafted scythes, the blade of which might have a length of 6 feet. At Threlkeld Hall, this type was used regularly to mow an area extending to almost 100 acres. Being soft ground, this field was unhandy for vehicles.

John worked at a farm at Castlerigg from which milk was taken to Keswick to be sold retail. There were forty-two cows to be milked by hand. The work began at 5 a.m. so that the milk 'lorry' might be ready in the yard before 7. He remembered using a churn for butter production. The mechanism became especially heavy just before the cream began to 'break'. After wartime service, John returned to Borrowdale—and to the larch woods. For a time he found employment in carting away timber from areas that had been savagely cleared. The timber, led by horses, was transported to the railway station at Keswick.

Jack Allonby, of Spark Bridge, making a besom.

The first car to be driven in Borrowdale belonged to the Simpsons of Hazel Bank. Bachelor John Simpson was a solicitor in Cockermouth. In the same house were three maiden sisters—Agnes, Sarah and Fanny. Other sisters had married and left their old home. John Hind drove the aforementioned car, a brand-new Argyll, brought from Newcastle in 1911, to and from his master's office, He had formerly been the coachman and gardener.

John recalled seeing a young couple who lived at a cottage 'up Langstrath'. The man earned money making heather besoms, which were sold at Keswick. Young men were fond of crossing the fells from Langdale so they might have a 'merry neet', with drinks, at the Royal Oak. On their return home one night they saw a Langstrath cottage—and a pile of bracken. They used some of the bracken to block the outside of the windows. The occupants of the cottage were not ruled by the clock; they worked when it was light and slept when it was dark. When some passers-by noticed the blocked windows and pulled away some of the bracken, the residents were 'terribly capped'. They said they must have slept 'two neets and a day'.

John Hind was married at the age of twenty-one. He and his wife found a home in Stonethwaite. It was well-named. John was working at Honister Quarry, beside the high pass. In the '80s and '90s immigrant workers had arrived from Wales and Cornwall. There was a Griffiths family from Wales. The Cornish families included men surnamed Brid, Spry and May. Four men—known as a 'company'—took on a contract for six months, providing their own tools and being paid so much per ton of dressed slate. At one time sixteen such groups worked at Honister.

The old ways ended in the 1930s, when the men agreed to have a bonus on output. The quarry-owners demanded 22 hundredweight to the ton so that breakages might be taken into account. Some men stayed up on the fell for a week. One man, named Gregg, remained there for four years, living in one of the huts provided. Just after the First World War, a Fordson tractor—a monstrous affair capable of hauling 14 tons—was purchased. It almost blocked the road, ran the risk of obstructing other road traffic and 'fair shook the houses as it went down the dale'.

William Hully, a Horse Man

I met William Hully at Bousefield, near Orton, in the 1950s. The major topic of conversation was horses. William, who had attended Brough Hill Horse Fair for over seventy years, described his home as being 'just on the division between two kinds of horse—Clydesdales and Shires'. At the time of our rural chatter he was eighty-eight years of age. William was nobbut a lad when he started riding horses. 'I started wi' nowt—an' no-one left me owt.'

When he came of age he found Comet, a stallion that weighed eleven hundredweight. That animal decided his career. It became an *entire*, which was an uncastrated animal used for breeding. William told me that he had led that animal for twenty years on the same piece of ground: 'Ere long he was serving over 160 mares a season.' Before the First World War, a good horse might be bought for between £40 and £50. William bought horses for the Army during that time. When the Armistice was declared he was in his 'second hundred'; the war had pushed the price up to over £100. Clydesdales were always popular in the Lake District—they did not have as much hair on their legs and therefore did not collect the dirt as much as a Shire horse.

Breaking in a horse for farm work took two or three months. The horse had to become accustomed to having a 'bit' in its mouth. It was then introduced to the saddle. Next in line were the tracings for work with implements. William Hully amused me by mentioning that when a saddle was to be involved a horse had to be introduced to something akin to that piece of equipment. An old pair of trousers, filled with straw, would be strapped to a horse's back. For tracings to be effective, an animal was yoked to a log to check on its ability to haul something. At the start of a new day horses were foddered by farm servants. They must be handy at the end of the working day to feed and groom the horses which were of the working type. Nowadays, a man just gets off a tractor and he's finished!

Thomas Longmire, Takking Hod

Wrestling in the Cumberland and Westmorland style has been a major feature at summertime sports meetings. My interest in the sport was stimulated when I visited a family friend called Longmire and stared for hours at a huge, glass-fronted case that occupied almost the whole of one wall, filled with trophies that 'our Tom' had won. It turned out to be a small part in the harvest of silver and leather that had been reaped by the son of a bobbin turner. He had won his first trophy in 1840.

Wrestling has attracted members of both sexes. Gentlemen like Christopher North had an active interest, and among the women who were attracted was a succession of Lady Lonsdales. They presented the trophies at Grasmere Sports. Those who excelled at wrestling in the Cumbrian style tended to be youngish men with muscles like bands of steel. They included farm lads, foresters and blacksmiths.

A wrestler wore a traditional four-piece costume, walking across lush turf in stockinged feet. The ring had no boards and no ropes; it was simply a stretch of turf, marked on three sides by the officials who observed the competitions. At Grasmere Sports the wrestlers had a broad arena framed by shapely mountains and with an enthusiastic crowd of spectators. When I first enquired about wrestling, the summer season lasted from May until October. Many wrestlers then took the sport indoors, at various academies; here the techniques might be polished until the return of bright weather. Meeting in the ring, the wrestlers shook hands, then each man placed his chin on the right shoulder of his opponent at the same time as grasping him around the back. If a hold was broken, the wrestler concerned had lost his bout, even though both men were still on their feet. One wrestler had a habit of soaping his back to gain an advantage. He was also terribly knock-kneed—another point in his favour. For a time the wrestlers moved around each other, their bodies low and their feet set well apart. One little man, benefiting from endless practice, proved himself to be equal to larger fellows.

Tom Longmire's reputation was such that both Wordsworth and Dickens penned pieces about him. When he visited Ferry Sports in 1857, Dickens referred to 'this quiet-looking giant' who had often been champion—'and will be so this day, although he is nearly forty and more than twelve years past the wrestler's prime'. He had never, in his twenty years' experience, been hurt. Dickens noted that Longmire 'won his first man's belt when a lad of sixteen years old'. Longmire was then living in New Hall Inn, Bowness, which was 'set in a wilderness of flowers'. Dickens had the wrestling technique displayed to him by Longmire, who showed the writer how to 'tak hod'. The occasion was well-remembered. Longmire had 'left his mark indelibly on our back, besides having compressed our ribs so that we cannot breathe right yet'.

Harriet Martineau,
a Neighbour of Wordsworth

Harriet Martineau was a radical who became the first English woman journalist of note. Born in Norfolk in 1802, the daughter of a wealthy manufacturer of French descent, she was to describe her unhappy childhood as her winter. She had been a sickly child. Bouts of ill-health were to recur throughout her life. Harriet designed and built herself a house, called The Knoll, at Ambleside. This new home was constructed during the winter of 1845. She had recently visited Palestine and Egypt.

Harriet's bright spirit enabled her to overcome ill-health, including deafness, and to leave, for our delectation, books, articles and pamphlets revealing a lively mind and thoughts that were about a score of years ahead of her time. Her interests ranged from the improvement of agricultural crops, against a background of potato famine in Ireland, to sanitation and building societies. A woman with an awesome intellect, Harriet penned a theological novel at the age of twenty-one. Matthew Arnold, who had a house at Under Loughrigg, was among those who were dismayed at Harriet's rejection of orthodox Christian beliefs, such as the notion of a personal God. He told a friend he had 'talked to Miss Martineau—who blasphemes frightfully'.

Harriet used her ear-trumpet like a microphone, directing it towards the people in the room. She was a popular and effective speaker. So many people turned up at the Methodist chapel in Ambleside to hear her lecture on domestic topics or on her distant travels that the building's partition wall had to be removed. Her speaking was, to one of her listeners, like the 'babbling of a brook and sensible, too'.

After the 'winter' of her unhappy childhood, the years of literary recognition became her stormy spring. The long summer of her life, when she lived in Ambleside, was undoubtedly a happy time, for it was during this period that she wrote what became her celebrated *Guide to Windermere*. For years my library held a battered copy of this 1854 work, printed by John Garnett—who operated from Windermere Post Office. I re-published this book in a list of Castleberg Books in 1995. The foreword, by Nigel Holmes, mentioned that I introduced the reader afresh to 'this large, robust woman with so kind, cheerful and intelligent a face'. A chapter is headed 'A Day on the Mountains'. A stranger had made three tours. Harriet considered 'there is one thing more he must do before he goes on into Cumberland. He must spend a day on the mountains: and if alone, so much the better.' The directions she gave may not legally apply today, but they have a certain mid-nineteenth century charm, which is why I like to read them. A stranger should 'come on to Ambleside by the early mail, and breakfast there. He must then set off up the road to the Nook, which anybody will show him.' The walker must be allowed to go forth early 'with a stout stick in his hand, provision for the day in his knapsack or his pocket and, if he chooses, a book but we do not think he will read today'. A map was essential to explain to him what he sees—'and it is very well to have a pocket compass, in case of sudden fog or any awkward doubt about the way'. Suggestions were made about the fell to be ascended; she decided it would be Fairfield.

The arrival of the railway at the hamlet of Birthwaite, soon to be known under the grand title of Windermere, had led to great physical and social changes. Harriet was the person who provided the necessary update. With the district entering its period of lusty Victorian growth, Harriet had felt that the first edition, with its quaint advertisements and tinted drawings, deserved a wider audience. The guide book (printed on a flatbed press) and her love of Lakeland were expanded into the *Complete Guide to the Lakes*. It took in aspects of the area in fine detail and was well-illustrated by drawings and maps.

The Knoll was subsequently divided into two, using traditional materials so it might fit cosily into a landscape of meadow and fell. Harriet used a large room as a study. It faced south and west and had two large windows. Multi-talented Harriet moved into her new home with a staff of two maids. Well-educated, having their own library, they were also given instructions on how to use a sewing machine. Visitors included George Elliot, Mrs Gaskell and Charlotte Bronte. The latter stayed with Harriet in 1850 and wrote a letter to Ellen Nussey in which she noted that Harriet's house was very pleasant, both within and without—arranged at all points with admirable neatness and comfort. William Wordsworth, aged seventy years, was a neighbour, his home being Rydal Mount, which stood one and a-half miles away. For four years, Harriet and William got on pretty well, despite her deafness. Wordsworth had false teeth that he often took out—when this happened, Harriet could not understand a thing he said!

Also living at The Knoll was Maria, a niece who did secretarial work and assisted with the running of a small farm. Maria wrote letters and copied out Harriet's books, an association that failed in 1864 when Maria died in her thirties of typhoid fever. Harriet suspected that she had 'picked it up' while nursing the sick.

Harriet's interest in rural matters took the form of a small book entitled *My Farm of Two Acres*. She had recruited a farmer from Norfolk to run the farm and attend to the two cows; a cottage was built for him. Wordsworth arrived to view the first calf that had been born. When the weekly wash was completed on Monday, the soap suds were used to bathe the pig she kept at the small farm near her home. She felt the pig was happier for being clean and, as a result, yielded better bacon. Harriet rose from her bed early in the morning, went for a walk before breakfast-time, then gave her maids their orders for the day. When she settled down to write no visitor was allowed to see her until the afternoon. She then walked again—with guests. Articles by the hundred—and a stream of profound books—flowed from her pen.

Harriet Martineau initiated social change. She founded a building society, and she lectured every Monday evening in the wintertime at the Methodist chapel in Rydal Road. She did not allow the gentry to attend the lectures, which ranged over many topics. They

Rydal Mount—the home of the Wordsworths in later life.

did not need educating and local folk must not be crowded out! She was often absent from Ambleside, travelling and lecturing. Her growing reputation as a writer gave her access to the political and literary coteries of London. She was, indeed, a notable individual, unconnected with a political party. Her politics were radical; she kept her own counsel, didn't greatly trust the Tories, and hated the Whigs. When Robert Owen tried to turn her into a socialist, she proved to be truly an independent thinker.

Harriet died in 1870. Despite her sharp manner and words, many of her Lakeland contemporaries were fond of her eccentricities.

23

Norman Nicholson,
Books and Plays

Norman Nicholson (1914–1987) was a poet of modern times who received the Queen's Medal for Poetry in 1977. He beheld the region in the spirit of Wordsworth and was usually thought of as a 'local poet'. Lovingly, refreshingly, he chronicled the various aspects of Lakeland as he experienced them. In the 1950s, when I first met him, I gathered from his reflective speech that the Lake District might become nothing more than a convalescent home for a sick urban civilisation! We chatted briefly at one of his art exhibitions.

As time went by I was inclined to visualise Norman as a solitary (though never lonely) figure with a setting on a grand scale—a sweeping mountain side. The *pruk, pruk* of a raven would be sounding though the mist, or in the amphitheatre of a Cumbrian estuary. Norman slowly, then positively, identified man and his works with the grand plan so that his home and the little town of Millom and its people—almost pure Victorian—became a part of it. In his writings he evoked stirring pictures of Millom, this small Victorian town, in its setting of sea, estuary and fell.

When I first saw Millom I had a feeling that most of the houses had been shunted into terraces. My first visit was on a spring day in 1968. The town was a-clatter with railway wagons. Groups of elderly folk wore unfashionable clothes—they might have stepped from Lowry paintings. They talked briskly among themselves in the minor canyons between the terraces. Norman's birthplace was No. 14 St George's Terrace, in the central part of the town. He was the only child of Joseph Nicholson, a local tailor and draper, and his wife, Edith Cornthwaite. She was the daughter of a butcher. Methodism played a part in their lives. Norman was educated locally but, alas, in the early 1930s he developed tuberculosis and was confined to a Hampshire hospital, losing one of his lungs through surgery. Norman spent most of his life at his birthplace and it was here that our first meeting took place. I was directed up several flights of steps to an attic bedroom, where, propped up in an iron-framed bed and resting against pillows, Norman was composing much of his perceptive prose and verse. A bout of flu had left him with a haggard look. He 'spoke' huskily, through a series of well-controlled belches that rendered his speech tonally soft.

Howard Spring would have written that Norman would have 'flared into the room'. He was wearing a brightly-coloured bed jacket that had been made for him by his wife, being a gift on his last birthday. Norman spoke quickly, coherently, interestingly—yet I

Norman Nicholson.

discovered that this celebrated Cumbrian author worked slowly, almost illegibly, with pen and stout paper. In winter he preferred to write while sitting up snugly in bed. He could trace the continued growth of the Terrace, which became a shopping area, with No. 14 as a chemist's shop. Norman found much to notice and write about with the grand view from the window of the attic, where he spent a good deal of his time. I enjoyed visiting it. The window was as rickety as was Norman after his strength had been sapped by illness. Standing beside it, I beheld a roofscape of slate beyond which, distantly, was the inscrutable form of Scafell Pike, the highest point in England. Norman preferred to look at the more-familiar Black Combe.

My last chat with Norman took place as we sat in the living room—a first-floor room of large Victorian size, its walls lined with books. I was shown an attractive framed photograph of Yvonne. She had taken part in an advanced course for producers under Martin Browne. One of the requirements was to produce a play; there was a choice of six, and Yvonne chose a scene from Norman's *Old Man of the Mountains*. They met to discuss the play, 'And that,' said Norman, 'is how I got to know her.' When he had married her in 1956, late in life, he had felt supremely happy. A Londoner, she had arrived in

Millom to teach, finding accommodation at the Vicarage. Her special talents were in speech and drama. Her terminal illness had been protracted and she died in 1982. They had no children.

It was clear from our talk that Norman was emotionally moved by Lakeland, its rocks and social history. He penned a book about impressions left by visitors to the Lakes during what had become known as the Romantic Age. Nearer home, he was moved by a landscape decayed by mining. Scarcely any feature escaped his notice. The meanest flowers were observed and commented on. He devised a play entitled *The Old Man of the Mountain*—on a cloudy day, he described it as having a bald, bleak forehead. 'So have I,' said he with a smile.

My last memory of Norman was when I was sipping tea at his fireside. The fire glowed. My rain-dampened trousers began to steam. The tea was 'China', sipped from a China cup. There was no milk, no sugar—just the true taste of tea against a glowing fire as dusk fell on a strange little town. The voice of Norman re-created life as it was in the 'good old days'.

Norman received a number of outstanding literary awards. In 1945 he was elected a fellow of the Royal Society of Literature; the OBE was conferred in 1981. Norman died in 1987. In April of the previous year, he had acknowledged the receipt of an advance copy of *Cumbria* containing the article I had written about our encounter. He noted:

> I am really very pleased with it. You have written in a most kindly and understanding way and I was very touched to read the references to Yvonne. And how much you observed! I knew you had a tape-recorder with you but I think you must have had a hidden cine-camera, too. If ever my house is burgled, I'll be able to use the article as evidence for the insurance.

Norman was original to the last.

Some years later I took a party from Abbot Hall, at Kent's Bank, to Millom. They were enchanted by the quaintness of the place and by a memorial window to Norman in the parish church. Norman—and his literary work—will never be forgotten.

24

John Peel, Huntsman and a Song

We remember John Peel (1777–1854) because of a song which portrays him as a huntsman whose coat was grey. The song was written by John Woodcock Graves, who knew Peel quite well but, in old age, was living in distant Tasmania. John Peel hunted foxes over half the county; the main area he covered was a triangle, with the points at Carlisle, Cockermouth and Penrith.

The Skiddaw group of fells lay within Peel's territory. The song about John Peel also mentions Low Denton Holme, which is near Caldbeck, and Scratchmere Scar, a little-known area east of Lazonby. The name John Peel is mainly linked with fell-country fells that are large, smooth, covered with bent, bracken, rush and heather in places. Here is a version of the first verse and chorus:

> *D' ye ken John Peel wie his cwote seay gray,*
> *D' ye ken John Peel at the breck o' day;*
> *D' ye ken John Peel gang far—far away,*
> *Wid his hounds an' his horn in a mwornin?*

> *For the sound of the horn cawt me frae my bed,*
> *An' the cry o' the hounds has oft me led.*
> *John Peel's view-hollo wad waken the dead,*
> *Or a fox frae his lair in a mwornin'.*

Peel was a dour, rather coarse man, his coarseness being fairly typical of his class and the age in which he lived. Like many another men at the time, his kidneys floated on nut-brown ale. Graves, by contrast, was eccentric, brilliant in some respects, passionate and quick-tempered. Like his idol Peel, Graves had little formal education. The song 'John Peel' was inspired by a tune, 'Bonnie Annie', which was a traditional Scottish rant or dance.

There are variations on how the song came to be written. I favour one that recalled a meeting between him and John Peel in a snug parlour at his home in Caldbeck. The two men had been remembering their hunting trips; Peel's mother was present, singing his baby to sleep with 'Bonnie Annie'. The pen and ink for hunting appointments were handy. The idea of writing the song forced itself on Graves, who jotted down the words of what would become 'John Peel'. Another version of how the song was created mentions an inn called The Rising Sun (which became the Oddfellows). '*D'ye Ken John Peel with his coat so grey?*' was considered to 'sing better' when Cumbrian dialect was used. When Graves sang it to John Peel, the huntsman smiled through a stream of tears. 'By jove, Peel,' added Graves, 'you'll be sung when we're both run to earth.'

Shortly after composing the song, Graves left Cumberland—there had been differences between himself and the manager of a Caldbeck woollen mill. He was fond of recalling John Peel, who died in 1854, aged seventy-eight. The song 'John Peel' was sung by men of the Border Regiment at the Relief of Lucknow. The present music, written by William Metcalfe in 1868, is based on an old Lakeland air.

As I continued to 'put people before things' as Editor of *Cumbria*, I was surprised to receive a letter signed John Peel. He turned out to be the great-great-grandson of the huntsman. In following years I often chatted with him at his home overlooking Lowther Park, near Penrith, and he gave me first-hand accounts of the lifestyle of Lord Lonsdale, who was also known as the 'Yellow Earl'.

He also gave me two verses of a hunting song I had not heard before:

> *The dawn is here, awake my lads,*
> *away, away.*
> *The mist has left the break, my lads,*
> *away, my lads, away.*
> *The clouds are rolling up the hill,*
> *O'er fairy dell and silver rill,*
> *Up frowning height and rugged hill.*
> *Away, my lads, away.*

A visitor to Queensborough cemetery, on the outskirts of Hobart, the capital of Tasmania, recalled seeing the gravestone reared in memory of John Woodcock Graves, 'who departed this life on the 17th of August, 1886. Aged 00 years'. Graves was, indeed, 91 years old when he breathed his last. He had enjoyed a happy and comfortable old age.

25

Beatrix Potter,
Her Life at Far Sawrey

Helen Beatrix Potter—to use her full name—was born in 1866 and died in 1943. She was a Londoner, being the daughter of well-to-do parents whose fortune had come from industrial concerns in Lancashire. In her young days, Beatrix was virtually a prisoner in a large, well-furnished house. Being closely chaperoned, she felt lonesome because her mother did not permit her to make friends with other children—they might bring germs into the house.

Beatrix was introduced to the Lake District through long summer holidays with her family at prime spots in the area. In the summer of 1896 the Potters rented, for a long stay, a mini-mansion called Lakefield at Near Sawrey, a lile village near Hawkshead. Children played on the local stretch of a frequently dusty main road leading to the Windermere ferry.

She bought nearby Hill Top, the cost being met by money received as royalties for her book about Peter Rabbit, plus a small legacy from an aunt. The main part of the house, which is now owned by the National Trust, is a joy to Potter enthusiasts. Hill Top became her retreat from an increasingly turbulent world. This property and the adjacent farmer's quarters were inter-connected; a door gave access from one kitchen to another.

Among those who visited her were Josephina and Delmar Banner. Josephine recalled for me that when they tapped on the house door there was a long silence. 'Then we heard little clogs toddling along on the flags beyond the door. They toddled up to the door, then stopped. 'We felt it was just like a little mouse, stopping to sniff the air, trying to detect who was coming.' The door was gradually opened—2 or 3 inches:

> We saw Beatrix's little face peep through the gap. She recognised us. She opened the door a little and said, 'Coom in.' And do you know what she was wearing on her head? It was an old-fashioned knitted tea-cosy, blue in colour. She looked so cute—like one of her dressed-up little animals.

In the second part of her life Beatrix was Mrs Heelis, wife of a shy Lakeland solicitor.   She had married William Heelis in 1913. She was forty-seven years of age. They settled down in Castle Cottage, which was, in effect, two cottages knocked into one and extended. The whole village might be scanned from a wide bow window. The garden was kept lush and weedy. A back staircase at her home was available if someone called at the main door

A drawing of Beatrix Potter.

and she did not wish to meet them. Beatrix would slip out of the house and retreat up a lane. During the courtship days, Appleby Willie (as he was locally known, from his origins) propped his motorbike behind a wall in the farmer's garden and strode on the last stretch to the home of Beatrix. After their marriage, Willie travelled by car to his office at Hawkshead, his progress being traceable because of his inclination to crash the car gears at the approach of every corner. Willie and Beatrix were fond of fishing from a flat-bottomed boat moored beside a local tarn they had stocked with trout.

Their house was kept in a primitive state, which was preferable. There was nothing smart, just bare flags, a scrubbed table and ordinary ladder-back chairs—yet everything was beautiful and clean. Beatrix was remembered as a small, dumpy, quirky character, also something of a skinflint. At dusk, in winter, a candle sufficed. Electricity was installed in the shippon. Perhaps the cows would like it!

Although best-remembered by many for her books, Beatrix was a dedicated farmer, with a particular love for the Herdwick, a sheep breed that evolved on the central fells. She had become aware of them during a family holiday at Fawe Park, Keswick, in 1903. Her enthusiasm for the breed developed through a family friendship with Canon Rawnsley, founder of the Herdwick Sheep-breeders' Association. She had appointed Tom Storey to rear sheep of good quality and took pride in attending Lakeland shows, drawing attention to her stock. Tom remarked, 'She didn't always identify the right pen of sheep!'

Her finest moments were when one of her sheep was awarded a trophy at a show. Beatrix kept the cups and allowed Tom to retain teapots and tankards. At Keswick Show she was photographed with Lady Leconfield, and she later talked her way to the sheep pens. Tom recalled for me that all the old-time sheep farmers knew her. 'She'd talk for a week with a real old chap who kept sheep.' Beatrix enlarged her stake in the Lake District, purchasing several dalehead farms with their stocks of Herdwicks.

She usually toured Lakeland in an antiquated, strange-looking black car that had similarities with a taxi. An old-time chauffeur was employed. When attending outdoor events, she often carried an umbrella that had belonged to Mr Warne, a partner in the publishing firm, to whom she might have been married but for his untimely death. Mr Warne had given her an engagement ring—it was lost in a hayfield.

Tom Storey worked for Beatrix as farm man and shepherd for eighteen years, then served under Mr Heelis for another two years. Tom's wife looked after Hill Top in winter and sometimes, going through the door, she would find Beatrix sitting quietly painting— or just thinking.

People I quizzed remembered her as a small, dumpy, somewhat quirky character. Amanda Thistlethwaite, of Hawkshead, who was six at the time, saw Beatrix walking down the road wrapped in sacks. 'She had a bit of a hat on. What a funny old woman.' Annie Black, another local lass, recalled Beatrix as 'a small lady, with rounded shoulders, silky white hair and fresh-looking face'. Beatrix shuffled along the surrounding roads with a round, cherubic face bent forward from rounded shoulders. Local people thought of her as an eccentric, distrusting the way she kept herself to herself.

She usually wore a costume of homespun Herdwick wool with two huge patch pockets at the sides. Her worsted stockings were of a kind of heather mixture. Quite often, an old straw hat was held firmly on her head by black tape tied under her chin. In her latter days, Beatrix used some sacking as a pinafore and clattered about in shiny black clogs!

Two years after the arrival of electricity in the village, a connection was made to Castle Cottage. She did not join the celebrations to mark an electrical link-up. They were held in the large barn at Sawrey Hotel in 1933.

Anthony Benson, shepherd, occasionally visited Castle Cottage but got no further than a chair just inside the kitchen. 'That is where you sat—about two paces in. She'd fetch you a cup o' tea and one meat sandwich; and that was that!' There was work a-plenty. Said he, 'A day wasn't lang enuff.'

William H. Waddington, an artist, was a tenant of Beatrix Potter, and he and his wife were neighbours. They saw her almost every day from 1916. When I chatted with William about Beatrix he recalled that she wore a tight little knitted bonnet. 'Her face had the complexion of a child's, with lovely rosy cheeks. She always looked alive and jolly.'

Beatrix had remarked that she liked the idea of an artist living next door, saying, 'He would not have a gramophone going in the garden…' I was surprised when I heard that some paintings, each measuring about 12 inches by 8 inches, had been wrapped in brown paper, with a blue ribbon. They were then left behind the geyser in the bathroom at Castle Cottage.

Hill Top, near Sawrey. (*Drawing by E. Jeffrey*)

I asked William Waddington about her artwork—she illustrated her animal stories with her own watercolour pictures. He replied:

> It was extremely good. Her drawings were most sensitive and beautiful. She also showed very clever draughtsmanship. Those illustrations were ideal for the purpose and she always made careful studies of the animals. Her drawings of them were anatomically perfect, being done from life.

Beatrix's writings—and the vivid illustrations that accompanied them—had a special appeal to children, yet I was told by more than one resident of Near Sawrey that children were somewhat scared by her strange appearance and manners. They were inclined to flatten themselves against a wall as she approached and run off after she had passed. This was indeed unusual considering her reputation among the most popular of children's story writers. Older folk, who noticed that she was socially indifferent, tended to regard her as eccentric. She was kind to local people in need.

Beatrix was fond of wandering. She wore the same heavy-looking, rather long, pepper-and-salt-mixture tweed coat and skirt and boots. The outdoors appealed to her even when she was ill. One day, confined to her bed through illness and temporarily having the house to herself, she slipped her husband's overcoat over her nightie and, with wellingtons on her feet, staggered into the garden to tug from the ground the last remaining Brussels Sprout stalk. Its lone presence had irritated her.

Anthony Benson, another shepherd employed by Mrs Heelis, first worked at Troutbeck Park as a lad fresh from school. He had been employed by a man called Isaac Fleming when he heard from Mr Heelis that a shepherd was needed at the Park. A meeting with Mrs Heelis was arranged. Anthony had been paid 25s a week. She offered him 50s 'straight off' and also built the Bensons a cottage. 'She kept us in coal. She fed five or six dogs.' The wage was as good as 60s. Anthony Benson was a shepherd at Troutbeck Park for fifteen years.

Beatrix lived through the early part of the Second World War; she would hear the wavering sound of engines on enemy aircraft as they headed for Barrow-in-Furness. A few hours before her death in December 1943, Tom Storey, her faithful shepherd, was at her bedside. He had been admitted to Castle Cottage. Willie Heelis was not at home. Beatrix lay in bed 'at yon end o' t'house'. There was no fire in the room. Tom recalled, 'I sat down and we chatted about farming. She asked how things were going on.' He left her at about 7 p.m. 'I hadn't stayed long. She died during the night.'

After her death, on 22 December 1943, Beatrix was cremated. This took place at Blackpool nine days later. Willie Heelis wrapped the casket containing her ashes in newspaper and delivered it, as arranged, to Tom Storey, her faithful shepherd. He finished his dinner and then left the house to scatter her ashes on higher ground, according to her confidential instructions.

Beatrix was most generous towards the National Trust, bequeathing to them over 4,000 acres and a number of farms. I recall with special clarity my last meeting with Tom Storey; arriving at his cottage home in Sawrey, I rapped my knuckles against the door and listened for his ever-bright 'Come in!' This time the response was delayed. Glancing through a window, I saw that his favourite chair was empty. He called faintly, inviting me to enter. Tom lay in bed, suffering from an old chest complaint. A few weeks beforehand he had mentioned his impending ninetieth birthday. I asked him about it. 'It's today,' he announced. Tom and I celebrated with glasses of sherry and chatted for a while until members of his family arrived with gifts and good wishes.

I thought of Beatrix as I walked up the quieter side of the Troutbeck valley, near Windermere. It is a valley flanked by the lean ridges of the fells that have gathered round High Street. Into view came that curious, huge lump of ground known as The Tongue. It is a squelchy area, its sides thick with bracken. Eventually, sitting down, I peered at Troutbeck Park farmhouse. Beatrix had bought the farm in 1923. She visited it fairly often in her chauffeur-driven car. A room on the ground floor was kept for her. I was told by Tom that she did not often go into the farm kitchen for a 'drink o' tea'. She had sandwiches, 'lapped [wrapped] in a piece of paper … She usually ate them outside.'

Arthur Ransome,
Swallows and Amazons

Arthur Ransome is famous the world over as an author of children's adventure stories. He made his name with *Swallows and Amazons*, which he set in his beloved Lake District. His usual writing plan—devising chapters, then writing the easiest first— was not followed on this occasion; *Swallows and Amazons* was completed in a single, inspirational surge, the tale being given a contemporary (late twenties) flavour rather than one that was historic. He typed at breakneck speed, using all his fingers. The pen-and-ink drawings that illustrated the book featured children, these images being adapted from photographs he had taken.

He wrote a dozen such books, his stories satisfying both his literary and boyish ambitions. Rupert Hart-Davis noted how the celebrated books were written—they were prepared by Arthur from an extremely detailed synopsis, complete with chapter titles. He knew exactly what was to happen in each chapter. 'He then began writing whichever chapter took his fancy or seemed easiest, leaving the most difficult to the last.'

Arthur, born during the last phase of the Victorian age, was the son of Cyril Ransome, an academic in Leeds whose spare-time passion was angling. Cyril and his family spent three summer months on vacation at the hamlet of High Nibthwaite, near the outflow of Coniston Water. As a boy, Arthur venerated the lake. On each visit he went through a 'special rite'; running across a field, he would crouch on the stone quay in order to dip a hand into the water. Swirling water marked what he considered to be his homecoming.

Ransome's literary ambitions dated from an early age. Born on 18 January 1884, he had listened attentively as his mother read aloud passages from such classics as *Robinson Crusoe* and *Treasure Island*. He experimented with various literary forms, but he was in his forties when success came, impulsively, with the writing of *Swallows and Amazons*, published in 1930. He blended childhood fantasies with real-life experiences.

The fictional crew-members of the boat *Swallow*—John, Titty, Susan and Roger—were based on the children of Ernest Altounyan, an Armenian-Syrian doctor who had married Dora, a daughter of the much-respected W. G. Collingwood. His stately home, named Lanehead, overlooked the head of Coniston Water. Needing a skipper of his fictional craft, Ransome turned Tacqui, the eldest child, into the boy named John. The *Swallow* was a one-time fishing boat 'monstrously heavy to row but not bad under sail'. It became the first of a long dynasty of such craft in his long sailing life.

The children, having explored the deserted little Peel Island (to use its actual name), settled into a happy routine of sailing, camping and fishing—until they came under attack from the Amazon pirates (Nancy and Peggy), who lived at Beckfoot and had not only visited the island but claimed that they owned it. Differences were settled in true English style—with an alliance, based on troubling the Blacketts' Uncle Jim. His temporary residence while he wrote a book was a houseboat anchored in a quiet bay; in *Swallows and Amazons*, he was dubbed a pirate by the name of Captain Flint.

Arthur was inspired by a scenic feature far removed from the Coniston-Windermere area where most of his celebrated book was set. He gave Friars Crag the name Darien and shifted it south so that the children of the book might camp where the promontory 'dropped like a cliff into the lake'—and there was a splendid backdrop of hills.

The urge to explore Wildcat Island (as it was known to Ransome) came to me with a drawing by Clifford Webb. It appeared in the first edition of *Swallows and Amazons*. The artist, using strong lines, pictured a secluded cove framed by large trees, with upsweeping rock in the background. A sailing dinghy, drawn up on the beach, was attended by three children—the Swallows, of course. Over sixty years had elapsed since, in the famous tale, John, Susan, Titty and Roger Walker sailed in the *Swallow* to camp on what they knew as Wildcat Island and encounter Amazons Nancy and Peggy. In 1994, a local man who had a boat classified as a sailing dinghy heard of my fascination with *Swallows and Amazons* and made it available to me. It was no longer adorned by a mast.

I was generously rowed to and from what is actually known as Peel Island. It is the property of the National Trust, and permission should be obtained for a visit. On the day of my visit, long years ago, the lake known as Coniston Water was flecked with silver light and strummed by a light northerly wind that gave clarity to the distant wooded shores of the lake and to some of the craggy fells around its head. Initially, we had an aerial escort in the form of two mute swans. During the voyage the only other craft to be seen on Coniston Water was the steamer *Gondola*, which operates a regular service to jetties around the lake and, like Peel Island, is owned by the National Trust. I occupied the stern seat of the dinghy and was not splashed when, as the boat was rowed across the lake, wavelets smacked their lips against the bows. An approach from the south-east was guaranteed to give me an element of surprise as Wildcat Island was suddenly revealed. The mute swans were now upending to dine on aquatic plants. Cormorants sped across the clear sky.

An inch of water lay between the well-laden boat and the shingle as we slipped between the headland and a rocky island sustaining a single tree. Ransome would have approved of this audacious course. I pondered on his boyhood at Nibthwaite and his boating and fishing on Coniston Water. He associated Peel Island with Wild Cats—and subsequently used the name *Wild Cat* for a schooner in *Peter Duck*.

Collingwood, in his novel about Thorstein (which proved to be an inspiration for Ransome), compared the island with a ship at anchor, adding: 'The little island is ship-like also because its shape is long and its sides are steep.' It has a high, short nab to the north which might be taken for a prow. A high sharp *ness* to the south might be thought of, in the same reckoning, as a poop. The 'long narrow calf rock' that Collingwood had compared with a cockboat at the stern of a ship was the spot from which I clambered into the dinghy for the return to the mainland.

During the outward voyage, the shape of the island had been slowly revealed. Jutting rocks, resembling pincers, created a well-sheltered landing place. The dinghy was beached and tied up to a tree. We followed well-used tracks. The northern end was not a place to linger in, being in shadow and strummed by a strengthening wind. The central valley—if a shallow depression might be so-called—evoked memories of W. G. Collingwood, who carried out excavations hereabouts, theorising that Norse settlers had used the place and being inspired to write *Thorstein of the Mere*—his best-known work of fiction.

Ransome made good fictional use of the main landing place on Peel Island. The plant life was profuse and varied. I recall a variety of trees, including (in addition to conifers) some indigenous species—oak, hazel and holly. Blackberries were there to be picked. Ling and bell heather grew rank—there were no browsing sheep to trim them. A snack meal was enjoyed in a sheltered spot on sun-warmed rocks. We scanned the mainland features—high hills, extensive woodland and, distantly, somewhere over Broughton Moor, a row of gigantic modern windmills. Happily, they were dwarfed by distance.

The *Esperance*, a craft used in the filming of *Swallows and Amazons*, had come into the possession of the Pattinson family in 1941. George Pattinson, who recalled seeing Arthur Ransome occasionally, took a great deal of interest in the filming by the BBC of his *Swallows and Amazons*. He told me that the boat was used in one production; when another film was made it was just a studio mock-up!

You can see Ransome's desk and typewriter in a room at Abbot Hall, Kendal. He wrote *Swallows and Amazons* in a bank-barn at Low Ludderburn. The lady who owned this property allowed me to visit the barn in which he had been photographed at work, his desk consisting of two tables that were set side-by-side. Standing beside the barn was a wooden garage where Arthur kept his car, a Morris Cowley, which he likened to 'a perambulating biscuit tin'. It enabled him to visit his childhood angling haunts.

Ransome's autobiography has a prologue and epilogue written by Rupert Hart-Davis, a great friend, who noted that Ransome was remarkable in many ways. He was made up of two different characters—half of him was a dedicated man of letters, with a passion for language and literature, and the other half was that of a perpetual schoolboy, complete with all the zest, fun, enjoyment and enthusiasm of youth.

Both aspects were satisfied when he sat at his desk in the bank-barn and, clatteringly, with an ancient typewriter, related Lakeland tales that charmed children and adults across the world. Arthur's last home was Hill Top, Haverthwaite; he died in 1967 and was buried in the churchyard at the head of the Rusland valley. The grave is marked by an inscribed stone of modest size.

27

Canon Rawnsley,
Watchdog of the Lakes

The spirit of Canon Hardwicke Rawnsley still broods over Crosthwaite Church. He was a powerful preacher, an incessant writer of sermons, poems and books about the Lake District. He was also one of the founders of the National Trust. He lived in sight of lofty fells—and his birth, in 1851, was in the flatlands of Lincolnshire. As a youngster, he had revelled in a healthy outdoor life, with a special love of angling and riding. Educationally, he progressed to Balliol College, Oxford, where he met John Ruskin and they became lifelong friends. His greatest fondness was for athletics, though he spent the first two years with Classics. His next ambition was associated with science; he considered taking up medicine as a profession. In the end he took Holy Orders, being ordained as a priest in 1877 and becoming Vicar of Wray, beside Lake Windermere. In the following year he married Edith Fletcher. A year later their only child, christened Noel, was born. It was on the instigation of Edith that the Keswick School of Industrial Art began, employing the leisure hours of working men and boys in the production of saleable objects fashioned from brass, copper and silver.

In 1882, Beatrix Potter came into the lives of the Rawnsleys. Beatrix, aged sixteen, was brought to Wray Castle for a holiday. She was in her teens when she met Rawnsley, the first published author she had encountered; he encouraged her to write what became her first book. In 1883, Bishop Goodwin of Carlisle offered Rawnsley the living of Crosthwaite, adjacent to Keswick. Wrote the Bishop, 'The vicarage, as you know, is simply charming. In my opinion, the post which I offer you is as near heaven as anything in the world can be.'

The induction took place on 8 July 1883. He tolled the bell sixty-four times and, after a short rest, a further forty-one times. At the vicarage, he carved in stone on the terrace wall some words written by Thomas Gray (1789):

> I got to the parsonage a little before sunset and saw in my [Claude] glass a picture that, if I could transmit to you and fix in it all the softness of its living colours, would fairly sell for a thousand pounds. This is the sweetest scene I can yet discover in point of pastoral beauty.

Canon Rawnsley enlivened his parish magazine with incidents of national importance. Other topics were re-housing, pure milk supply and how to prevent tuberculosis. In 1888, on behalf of the Wordsworth Society, Rawnsley caused two verses from Wordsworth's elegiac poems to be engraved on the Brothers' Parting Stone. The lines had been composed in 1805 in memory of a sad parting five years earlier. William and Dorothy Wordsworth had turned back for home at Grasmere. William's brother, Captain John Wordsworth, went on to Penrith, thence back to sea. He perished when his ship was wrecked in Portland Bay. What became known as the Brothers Parting Stone is situated about 100 yards from Grizedale Tarn:

> *Here did we stop; and here looked round*
> *While each into himself descends*
> *For the last thought of parting friends*
> *That is not to be found.*

> *Hidden was Grasmere's Vale from sight,*
> *Our home, and his, his heart's delight,*
> *His quiet heart's selected home,*
> *But time before him melts away*
> *And he hath feeling of a day*
> *Of blessedness to come.*

Rawnsley grew to love the high hills, especially those around Keswick and Grasmere. In his later years he penned books reflecting joyfulness in high and lonely places. Rawnsley held his living at Wray for five years. In 1891, he became a Canon of Carlisle Cathedral, received more honours, visited Moscow in 1896 for the Coronation of the Czar and continued to write prose and poems, including 'A Song of Spring':

> *Come! Sweet April, whom all men praise;*
> *Bring your daffodils up the Raise,*
> *Bid the delicate warbler trill,*
> *Come with the cuckoo over the hill*
> *Sprinkle the birch with sprays of green,*
> *Purple the crops all between;*
> *Bend the rainbow and swell the brooks,*
> *Fill the air with the sound of rooks,*
> *Rubies lend, for the larch to wear,*
> *The lambs are bleating, and May is near.*

In 1917 he retired to Grasmere, having purchased Allan Bank, which had Wordsworthian associations. Rawnsley died at Allan Bank in 1920 and was interred at Crosthwaite. Clara Boyle, the source of many stories about Lakeland personalities, was fond of recalling her first meeting with Canon Rawnsley; the year was 1914, by which time he was a celebrity and, said Clara, 'very much the central figure in Lakeland.' In conjunction with Octavia

Hill and Sir Robert Hunter he had founded the National Trust. Initially it was concerned with protecting open spaces and a variety of threatened buildings. Over the years the Trust has benefited from numerous donations of both property and money, and it now owns over twenty features throughout Cumbria. These range from areas of beauty such as Borrowdale and Ullswater to Sizergh Castle and the *Gondola* on Coniston Water. Hardwicke Rawnsley has left a great legacy.

28

Will Ritson,
the Complete Dalesman

Statesmen were men who lived on a landed estate, and, by tradition, they led quiet, almost unchanging lives among the great fells. They were, in the main, a thoughtful, taciturn lot—warm-hearted among themselves but terribly offhand and reticent with strangers. Then, in the first decade of the nineteenth century, when the statesman tradition was beginning to wear thin as a consequence of social changes and an inflow of new faces, a great noise rang out in Wasdale, the wildest and most westerly of the Lakeland valleys. Will Ritson had arrived.

Will was born at Row Foot in 1808. When he was still a small boy he remonstrated with the local parson as baptismal water was sprinkled on his forehead. Through Will Ritson, the 'statesman' tradition would be bolstered. Will added a wing to the family home of Row Foot, transforming it into an inn. Rough but brilliant, he was eventually to be known with some affection as 'Auld Will' and become a major attraction to the area. He was sought after especially by literary folk, who enjoyed his manner, recollections and comments, which were delivered with a dry wit. He was capable of speaking in Queen's English—and might also make a remarkable play with Lakeland dialect.

Auld Will was in the mind of most of the folk who took the winding road to Wasdale Head, passing close to Wastwater, the least changed of the major lakes since they were formed in the Ice Ages. Wastwater has a cold, blue appearance, implying there is little life. Extensive Screes, on fells just beyond the water, resemble huge grey fans. Auld Will claimed that Wastwater was the deepest lake in England. He was also proud to live within sight of Scafell Pike, the English high spot, its topmost crags being at an elevation of 3,210 feet above sea level. The highest peak in the land is much less obvious from the dale than is the lofty pyramid of Great Gable, which would become the symbol of the Lake District National Park.

Auld Will's oft-repeated claims for his birth dale extended beyond those for the deepest lake, the highest mountain and the smallest church. Wasdale Head had the biggest liar—himself. The lies he told were not malicious—'They're nobbut big exaggerations.' Will was fond of recalling a local farmer who, asked by a lad on top of a haystack the best way to get down, shouted, 'Shut thee e'es an' walk aboot a bit.'

He tended Herdwick sheep and 'took hod' in wrestling contests. With the coming of autumn he was quite prepared, with others, to leave work or wife when the sound of a hunting horn roused the echoes. He became huntsman to Mr Rawson, of Wasdale Hall, and later to a Mr Huddleston.

Diane, his wife, was unlike him in manner, being quiet and retiring. She became a perfect partner; behind her unexciting demeanour there was an industrious nature. Wasdale Head has changed remarkably little in appearance or population since Auld Will's time, though his home has grown out of recognition. Tourism began in the 1840s— prior to this date, the valley housed a lost race of almost pure Vikings.

Auld Will was latterly tall and grey, his frame being lightly covered with flesh and skin. An aquiline nose was in the best Viking tradition. He grew old with dignity and died in 1890 at the age of eighty-three. A great silence seemed to descend upon Wasdale, where his tongue had ceaselessly chattered with words and phrases that had been well-used in the dale for generations.

29

Cedric Robinson, Queen's Guide to the Sands

My first association with Morecambe Bay, to the south of the Lake District, was as a child, on a family holiday, making sandcastles on a beach that seemed to be a blend of sand and mud. Years later, visiting the Bay with a friend, I made the error of describing the sandy areas as being dead and desolate. He disagreed. A thin, dark cloud, racing low over the sand, was made up of hundreds of wading birds. Hard, grey rocks were the remnants of moraines of boulder clay left by Ice Age glaciers, and now tenanted by mussels and conger eels.

My friend Dr F. W. Hogarth, who had studied life on and around the Bay intently, believed that the curious duplication of the vowel sound in local names denoted a Norse origin. *Craam* was an iron rake. *Laaster* was a three-pronged fishing spear. *Haaf*, a large hand-net, was used for taking salmon and sea trout. The name Morecambe is said by some to have a Celtic derivation, this being *Myr-cym*, meaning Crooked Sea. To the Romans it was *Aesturarium Moricambris*. The travellers in Wordsworth's time (1770–1850) used the sands as a handy route to Furness and West Cumberland. It was more direct, less tedious, than inland ways.

Wooden poles, standing firm against the tides and river currents, formed a baulk used for fishing—a so-called 'fixed engine' which, if properly set and maintained, might yield as many fish as a deep-sea trawler. I walked near the Central Pier at Morecambe. It cast a shadow over Morecambe trawlers I saw regularly; they were unlike the sturdy fishing cobles of the turbulent East Coast, having the graceful lines of yachts and being very much at home on the shallow, sheltered Morecambe Bay. Wordsworth wrote:

> The stranger, from the moment he sets foot upon these Sands, seems to leave the turmoil and the traffic of the world behind him; and crossing the majestic plain when the sea has retired, he beholds, rising apparently from its base, the cluster of mountains among which he is going to wander, and towards whose recesses … he is gradually and peacefully led.

Described as 'a big inner sea' and as 'a wet Sahara', the Bay might look shallow but the tidal range—between 20 and 30 feet—is impressively large. A tidal-bore invades the Kent estuary at up to 9 knots, the speed of a good horse, disappearing amid a flurry of foam against the iron columns of a railway viaduct, set on a firm base below 70 feet of sand.

Salt water runs up the gutters, performs pincer movements around the sandbanks (which it softens before overwhelming them), bubbles and boils about the *skeers* and spreads over several thousand acres of inter-tidal marsh. A cross-sands walking route remained in regular use until 1857, at which date a railway line was opened twixt Carnforth and Ulverston.

Birdwatchers love the sandy expanses of Morecambe Bay. Years ago I spent many hours with binoculars studying the avian population. Shelduck waddled over the ground, at the edge, raising their young in burrows. The winter tideline echoed to the calls of wading birds such as curlew and lapwing. Arriving in spring were fleeting hosts of migrant birds—knot and dunlin, turnstone and godwit—northward bound to their nesting haunts. They would be back on the Bay in the autumn, darkening patches of sky and casting shadows over glistening sands. The wailing cry of a Great Northern Diver might be heard, or there might be a glimpse of a Red-throated diver.

Horse and cart fishermen from Flookburgh on Morcambe Bay at low tide.

Heading for the Lake District across the sand and mudflats of low-tide Morecambe Bay was considered a proof of good taste. George Fox, founder of the Society of Friends, knew the Sands of Morecambe Bay. He travelled this way to and from the home of the Fell family at Swarthmoor Hall, near Ulverston, premises which were later to be thought of as the birthplace of Quakerism. Of commercial interest to blue-ganseyed men who went to the Sands with horse-drawn, two-wheeled carts, were cockle, mussel, shrimp and fluke. Massed cockles were reportedly heard 'singing', a faint sound compared with the pattering of light rain. They were gathered when brought to the surface of the wet sands by a device—wooden boards on two long handles—known as a 'jumbo'. Shrimps were harvested during a season extending from March until the onset of the first frosts. Ashore, they were boiled, then 'picked', being prepared for sale.

I had long chats with William Burrows, who was employed by the Duchy of Lancaster as guide to the shifting sands. William had been walking, sailing and fishing in Morecambe Bay for rather more than seventy years. Times and conditions change. The Bay has silted. He could remember when as many as five steamers and forty yachts had tied up or were near a pier in August. The pier, with three tiers, existed before the promenade was constructed. William told me that you were charged a penny for treading on its wooden planks. William became official guide for the sands, which, at low tide, might be crossed between Hest Bank and Kents Bank. At one time or another, he had guided all sorts across the sands—there had been babes in arms and blind people. In due course, Cedric Robinson combined cockling and fishing in the Bay with his ancient duties as Sands Guide, leading groups of people from shore to shore.

Guides had come into prominence with the establishment of the priories of Cartmel and Conishead. Cedric, like William, has done the work of guide for the Duchy of Lancaster, occupying the old Guide's Cottage near Grange-over-Sands. Familiarity with the Bay did not breed contempt. The precise route depends on the course taken by the River Kent, the swiftest river in England. The route is possible for only half a day; at other times it is covered with swirling water.

In 1986, Cedric collaborated with me when I was compiling *Life Around Morecambe Bay*, a picture book with a foreword contributed by the Duke of Edinburgh. Cedric sat beside the Duke in 1975 when he headed a cavalcade of horse-drawn carriages across the sands before visiting Holker for the Horse Driving Trials. Having seen Morecambe Bay from the air, the Duke was now able to experience the full beauty of the Sands in their setting of Lakeland hills, 'and to experience the very special atmosphere of that unique place'.

The weather varies. A storm broke out with dramatic suddenness when he was leading a party of visitors by a sands way to Chapel Island, in the estuary of the Leven. The walk began in glorious weather at the appropriately-named Sandgate. Cedric told me, 'We set off wearing next to nothing. I was a little more sensible and carried a jersey over my arm. When we began the return walk it was still a beautiful day.' A quarter of a mile away from *terra firma*, Cedric heard a noise that was like an approaching tide or a steam-hauled train on the Furness railway line. A storm was coming up the bay:

Cedric Robinson, Sands Guide, leads the way towards the Kent Estuary.

The rain that hit us was like bullets, fast and fierce. All the marks left in the sand had been rubbed out. What had been dry sand suddenly became about 2 inches of sodden sand. Everything merged into one.

There were flashes of lightning. Cedric blew his whistle, but it didn't make much difference:

We had broken up into three groups, each holding hands and walking head down. What seemed like an age was only a matter of minutes. The storm passed. The whistle was blown afain. We all got together—and talked about our frightening experience.

Back at the house at Cart Lane, Cedric's wife had watched the storm in comfort while washing clothes. She hung them out to dry. 'One moment the washing was limp. The next moment it was being blown high in the air. I could hardly get it off the line.'

Grange-over-Sands offers a handy approach to Cartmel, which is dominated by an outstanding Priory. Up to the time of the Romantic Movement in the middle of the eighteenth century, the Cartmel area was probably the most isolated part of England, being almost surrounded by water. To the north are the great hills of Lakeland, and westward and eastward are the estuaries of Kent and Leven. From the eighteenth century, Cartmel became a 'stepping stone' used by students of romantic beauty, from Gilpin to Wordsworth and his contemporaries.

30

John Robinson, the White House

Appleby-in-Westmorland is situated in a loop of the River Eden. The glowing red sandstone of Edenvale has been used so commonly in buildings that it sometimes gives a glow to the underbellies of passing clouds. One notable building was plastered over and painted white. I refer to the White House in Boroughgate, built by the affluent Lowther family in the mid-eighteenth century. At the time of my visit it was the residence and medical centre of Dr Peter Delap. Several hundred red deer ranged across some of the quieter fells. Roe deer inhabited deciduous woodland at lower levels. Peter, a founder member of the British Deer Society, had developed the art of being inconspicuous in manner and clothing.

I loved to visit the loft at the White House, where a vast number of cast deer antlers were neatly arranged. Roe deer sometimes appeared in the White House back garden. There was a time when, as I waited for people to remain, I wandered into the back garden, which was adjacent to a steep-side reach of the local beck. I sat quietly. Emerging from the wooded environs of the Eden for a snack was a roe deer. It was attentive for a while before settling down to feed.

The White House was built at the expense of John Robinson. The son of an Appleby apothecary was to rise from humble circumstances to social heights; at a time when patronage was a key to commercial success, he was befriended by the Lowthers, becoming their man at Appleby. With bigger ideas in mind, Jack Robinson moved to London in 1780. One of his commendable tasks, during his climb to prominence, had been making arrangements for oak trees to be planted in the Great Park at Windsor.

Tufton and Lowther were two families of local significance. The Lowthers, anxious to extend their influence in Appleby, arranged for the house to be built. Their own man would be in residence. Such a move, they felt, would give the Tuftons a run for their money. John Robinson, who had been apprenticed to a Penrith solicitor, was, at the age of 26, tempted back to Appleby. He persuaded the Lowthers to let him build a fine house. One day, as I discussed this with Peter Delap, he said, 'For a start, his ambitions seemingly outran the Lowthers' plans for him.'

In Victorian times the White House was a girls' boarding school. It became the residence and surgery of a doctor when the job was held by Dr Bell, then Dr Sprott, followed by Dr Fowli. The Delaps bought The White House from the Hothfield estate in the 1950s. Hanging on a landing was a copy of a portrait of the aforementioned John

Robinson—'a man with a plump, bland but essentially hard face, the archetypal Mr Fix It. In those days of poor communication and hard travel, able agents could prosper exceedingly.'

The White House needed a small army of servants. Being kept in attic rooms, they shivered in winter and sweated profusely in summer. There was no shortage of domestic works. In its heyday, the number of coal fires to be serviced was twenty-two. Three of them were in outbuildings. About ten years after he set up the house some garden houses were built. In Peter Delap's day, one of the houses became a deer museum. Said he, 'An interest in deer can keep a person in a stressful job sane. He can run away and hide in the bushes! He just falls back into the Paleolithic.'

31

H. W. Schneider and
the Steam Yacht *Esperance*

The Schneider family, natives of Switzerland, settled in England during the eighteenth century, becoming respected London merchants. They had an interest in mining, which was undertaken at home and abroad. Henry William Schneider, born in London, had the family flair for business. He visited the Lake District in 1839, ostensibly on holiday, and subsequently transformed the village of Barrow, beside Morecambe Bay, into an industrial town! His nimble mind and zestful manner led to a rapid expansion of the iron-ore business in Furness.

This giant of the Industrial Revolution married Augusta Smith, the daughter of a mine-owner. The marriage lasted for twenty years. She died after bearing Henry three sons. Marrying for a second time in 1864, his bride was Elizabeth, daughter of Canon Joseph Turner, who was Vicar of Lancaster. She bore him four daughters and died when the Schneiders were holidaymaking on the continent.

Schneider had a London home but eventually became a man of two north-country worlds—the stressful business and public life of Barrow and the more languid retreat at a home established at Belsfield, overlooking Bowness Bay on Windermere. This mansion, of Italianate style, had been built for the Baroness de Sternberg; it was greatly embellished by the Schneiders. In 1874, *The Westmorland Gazette*, commenting on Belsfield, noted:

> …nothing could be finer than the prospect from the south and west on the terrace, where the eye catches a glimpse of Bowness and stretches far over the lake to the opposite shore, affording every diversity of surface, hill and hollow for which the district is famed.

Eight acres of ground were floriferous, adorned with 'glass houses'. Two conservatories (one of them 30 and the other 45 feet long) were built in which to grow peaches; they would not otherwise have flourished. An azalea-house was a span-roofed structure 54 feet by 18. It was used for growing plants that decorated the conservatory. A railway connected Lakeside, close to the outflow of Windermere, with up-and-coming Barrow, where Schneider had his office. Schneider, being one of the directors of the Furness Railway, had a special coach on the Barrow train. A secretary was at hand. Business-like, Schneider was exploiting a rich field of haematite ore in the Furness district.

Schneider ordered from Clydeside a steam-yacht named *Esperance*, which would take him from his home to the railway. The yacht, 75 feet in length, had a hull of high-grade

H. W. Schneider, the Furness industrialist. (*Drawing by Richard Bancroft*)

iron and twin screws. Constructed by T. B. Seath & Co. of Rutherglen, near Glasgow, the *Esperance* sailed from the Clyde to Barrow. Railway wagons were adapted to convey the craft to Lakeside, where, in the March of 1870, she slid gently on to the lake, being much-admired. The engines were of a compound type, with single-cylinder block and two sets of inclined pistons forming an inverted V. Connecting rods were linked with each shaft. Crewed by two men, *Esperance* cruised the 7 miles to Lakeside in less than an hour.

Early on a working day, when Schneider walked on paths through the Belsfield gardens, he was preceded by his butler, Mr Pittaway, who carried breakfast on a silver tray. They boarded the *Esperance*, which had a crew of two men, and had a pleasant lake cruise, reaching a railway station at Lakeside in less than an hour.

The Schneider phase was to be the most elegant in the life of the steam-yacht. After his death, the craft was hauled out of the water south of Cockshott Point. Four years elapsed before Bruce Logan, of the Ferry Hotel, bought the craft and used her to ferry people and goods between the hotel and Bowness. On Sunday morning, hotel guests sailed in her to attend church at Wray. She was popular, and regained some of her lost grandeur. *Esperance* was known to Arthur Ransome, a notable writer—she appeared as a houseboat in *Swallows and Amazons*, one of his best-known books.

In the summer of 1958 I had an opportunity of cruising in the *Esperance*. A small but durable fibre-glass rowing boat carried us out to the notable vessel; the 'old lady' of Windermere lay moored in Rayrigg Bay, near Bowness, with a foot of water under her black hull of rustless iron. She had a neat and perfect design, preserved by her owner, G. H. Pattinson, a member of one of the oldest families in Bowness. She had been allowed to keep her basic appearance. The heart still beat strongly, although she was powered by a petrol engine instead of being steam-driven. Into the slim black funnel were directed exhaust fumes from her two four-cylinder Ford engines, which developed 49 horsepower. In the funnel was a device for producing steam. Quite soon she was free of her moorings, and, with one engine ticking over, headed smoothly from the bay. Her raked stem took spirit out of wavelets created by a gusty wind. It fascinated me to learn that for something like ninety years she had faced storm and sunshine on Windermere without any loss of dignity.

There were faster boats on Windermere. Noisy speed-boats darted among other craft. Some of them were pulling skiers. Large cabin cruisers, half-cabined craft from Bowness Bay, held hordes of excited holidaymakers. I even saw one or two canvas canoes. *Esperance* claimed most of the attention, however, especially when Mr Pattinson took her close inshore at Bowness to show me the original pier against which she was moored; it was still known as the *Esperance* Pier. Dozens of cameras began to click, and hundreds of friendly hand-waves acknowledged that the craft on which I had been sailing was something special.

32

W. T. Shaw, A Miner's World

At its peak rather more than a century ago, Lakeland mining employed 1,000 men. A Lakeland miner had a chancy occupation; he was at the whims of the market. When the price for materials fell and mines were closed, he must be prepared to go elsewhere. A lot of men went from Coniston to America. Some returned, but many stayed in the New World.

The Lakeland world of W. T. Shaw was that of the mine—deep, dark, dank, but exciting to those who devoted themselves to the discovery of and extraction of minerals. Members of his family were miners for several generations. He was born at Coniston in 1909. At that time, the village was only half its present size. Mr Shaw attended Coniston School along with about a hundred other children. Coniston was best-known for its copper mines. A French company operated there prior to the First World War; their interest ended when the war broke out. The intention had been to open the mines in a big way. The major source of employment was slate-quarrying, the largest quarry—on the face of Coniston Old Man—being owned by the Mandale brothers, who employed around 100 men and boys. Slate of a light colour, wrenched from the Old Man, found a good market in Lancashire towns.

Slates were transported from the district by train, being delivered to the station on horse-drawn carts. During the First World War another considerable export was timber, much of it big, mature stuff felled on the Marshall estate. Coniston was reasonably prosperous; the slate quarryman made a fairly good wage, in the context of the wages of the period. Working on contract, they were paid about £2 according to the quantity of slates produced. Small gangs—each of four men—reached mutually satisfying arrangements with the agent.

Mr Shaw's working life began at Greenside, Ullswater, where he was apprenticed to the old manager, William Henry Borlase. Greenside at that time employed 100 men and boys. Underground work had reached a depth of 120 fathoms (237 fathoms when, in due course, the mine was closed). Greenside was the economic mainstay of Glenridding. Almost every able-bodied man worked at the mine. Nearly every house took in a lodger.

Mr Shaw's first job was at the crushing mill, where he 'watched' the concentrating tables at which the lead ore was washed. For a time he trained with an engineering firm in Glasgow. Work at Greenside extended from 7 a.m. to 4.30 p.m. (noon on Saturday), with the underground workers engaging in eight-hour shifts. As the workings were extended, there was a progressively longer walk to the points of activity.

In the mid-1920s, economic conditions were good, and there was work for everyone. Gradually, the price received for lead fell away. The mine was closed, and Mr Shaw left in 1931. There was a humane system under which the single folk, or those with few dependents, went first, leaving the married men to work as long as possible. Mr Shaw remembered when underground workers strode cheerfully along the levels, clad in old clothing and with no hard hats or other special devices concerned with safety.

Everyone wore clogs, then wellingtons became the general rule. In the pre-wellington days, miners had not wanted to get their feet wet early in the shift. The gutters beside the levels were kept clear and drainage was good. Later, miners slopped along through the water. The lead ore was taken away in steam wagons and put on the rails at Troutbeck for Newcastle, where it was smelted. There were two steam engines—a Foden, then the new Sentinel, which could carry 10 tons of material comfortably. Coal for the engines and other purposes was brought in to Troutbeck by rail.

33

Short Brothers, Boats that Flew

During the Second World War, Sunderland flying boats, assembled by the east bank of Windermere, were flown off the lake to form part of Coastal Command. I was fortunate to see one of these monster aircraft take to the air—it was awe-inspiring. I was a Boy Scout on a camping trip not far from Windermere, undertaking my first-class journey. I had to be away from the camp for twenty-four hours, having next to nothing to eat and only a large square of waterproof material under which to shelter.

I had dined well at the camp site. Rabbits were on the menu—thanks to a visiting farm lad and his ferret. One of the joys of leaving camp had been that I escaped the task of skinning rabbits. I strode joyously towards my first objective, this being the ferry-landing just south of Bowness, from which I could sail to a point near Ferry House. Two long cables stretched 720 yards across the lake. The cables kept the ferry boat on a fixed path across the water. After its six-minute voyage, the ferry touched the shingle, a ramp was lowered and a man clad in blue overalls raked the shingle to give smooth passage for vehicles from ferry to shore. I stepped ashore to move up a steep hill leading to Sawrey.

The ferry was a coal-fired job, with a slight list on the side where the engine was situated. It was operated jointly by Lancashire and Westmorland County Councils. John Hoggarth, of Far Sawrey, remembered when the ferry was a large rowing boat, with four men to do the rowing. If horses and carts were being transported, the horses were taken out of the shafts to conserve space.

During the short Windermere voyage, I beheld the cherry-red fire, heard the hiss of escaping steam and then—wait for it!—a loud droning sound to the north. The Sunderland flying boat, all four engines in lusty action, was taking off from the lake. As it passed it seemed to cast a shadow over half the district.

Forty years later, while conversing with the aforementioned George Pattinson, founder of the Windermere Steamboat Museum, I heard more about Windermere's special contribution to the war effort. Cooper Pattinson, the father of George, was a pioneer of flying boat development in the First World War, being awarded the first DFC for shooting down a Zeppelin after pursuing it in a F2A flying boat. The Zeppelin was brought down over the Heligoland Bight.

Father was friendly with Francis Short, one of two brothers who manufactured the Sunderland flying boats. He had been allowed to board the first of these monster aircraft assembled at a wartime factory beside Windermere. Factory workers and their families were housed in an adjacent settlement known as Calgarth Estate. The first Windermere Sunderland had taken from lake-water to air in 1942. Lancaster Parker, the chief test pilot for these aircraft (which were classed as military), allowed Cooper to take one set of controls, which he held as the huge craft took to the air. Asked where he would like to go, Mr Pattinson mentioned some property in Great Langdale. The Sunderland flying boat, low in the sky, traversed the dale, turning over Blea Tarn and returning to base over Little Langdale. This flight must have caused consternation among local folk and the indigenous sheep.

George Pattinson, home on leave from the Royal Navy, watched the flying boat touch down safely. He was familiar with the wartime role, having served on convoy-escort duties. In 1988, while walking on the shore of Windermere, I had a bad attack of nostalgia—and appeased it by seeking out his astonishing collection at the Windermere Steamboat Museum.

34

Graham Sutton,
a Writer at Dancing Beck

Graham Sutton, a native of Scotby, near Carlisle, came from a family who were well-rooted in Cumbria. They owned farmlands and a tannery. Educated at St Bees School, he became Head Boy, leaving in 1911 to go to Queen's College, Oxford, where he took an Honours degree in English. Graham also treaded the boards as an actor at Stratford-on-Avon; he had a spell of teaching at Edinburgh Academy. He gave a high priority to national service, being a despatch rider in the First World War and serving in the Home Guard during the Second.

Graham was tall, powerfully built, but quietly spoken, and had a deep love of Lakeland. He felt it was as much a part of him as his heart and sinews or, as he would be more likely to phrase it, his 'liver and lights'. That love of his native land was forthright and cheerful. He is best remembered for his novels about the Flemings, a Lakeland family who had kept sheep since 1706.

Some of the many short stories he penned had Lakeland settings. I recall in particular a tale headed *The Man Who Broke the Needle*. There was a rock-climbing element; Graham enjoyed climbing crags. I heard that friends of his who were new to the fells were liable to be enticed by Graham to the practice slabs near a farm in Borrowdale, and 'shown how'.

In July 1954, he and his wife bought *Dancing Beck*, a new home; included in the purchase was a good deal of land at Underskiddaw. He arranged for a bell to be hung in the entrance hall—that bell had belonged to his father, William Sutton of Scotby, and it had a most resounding tone. It had been intended to catch the attention of various employees of William Sutton by different numbers of workers.

Graham was an accomplished writer who also maintained a well-equipped workshop, where he turned out additions to his furniture in leisure-time twixt 'books and plays'. He was fascinated to discover how things worked and bubbled over with ideas for stories, plays and novels. Graham had a wide range of talents including watercolour paintings, woodwork and repairing a grandfather clock. He had constructed the desk at which he wrote. He carved an image of the head of Sir Walter Raleigh upon the bowl of a pipe that had been presented to a friend.

The first Graham Sutton book I read was *Fell Days*. It was created from broadcast talks and was a most enjoyable read. The Fleming family featured prominently in his work. Books entitled *Shepherd's Warning, Smoke Across the Fells* and *North Star* carved for him a niche in the literature of the Lake District. The aforementioned *Fell Days*, a book of essays, incorporated much of the raw material from which these novels were shaped in the form of antiquarian studies.

Eventually, over twenty books bore his name. He also wrote plays that were transmitted by the BBC. I found pleasure, when visiting the area he knew and loved, in glancing at a summer house where he jotted down these fascinating tales. I met his widow; she died at the ripe old age of ninety-two.

35

Alfred Wainwright, Fell Walker Extraordinary

To Alfred Wainwright, Lakeland was heaven. The television series *Coronation Street*, with its rich assembly of characters, was a reminder of where that road to heaven had begun—in a Lancashire milltown. 'AW', as he was popularly known, grew up in Blackburn, a man-made environment of mills and terraced housing. A red-haired lad, he lived in a two-bedroomed, mid-terrace house in Audley Range, with a view across the road of the local brickworks.

AW had an unhappy childhood. Albert, his father, was a stonemason from near Penistone. He was remembered by a cousin as 'charming when sober but garrulous and coarse when drunk'. When he was in a drunken condition, Albert would insist on one of his daughters playing him the hymn 'Lead Kindly Light' on the piano. The Wainwrights would have been a happy family if his father had not introduced 'the cursed drink' into the house.

Emily, his God-fearing, chapel-going mother, raised four children. She kept the family going 'on next to nowt' and had the main share in the bringing up of the children. Alfred, born in 1907 to a family living in the main part of town, was a tiny baby with dark, shiny eyes and light hair. This was unusual for the Wainwrights.

Mum went out cleaning and took in washing to help meet the household running costs, including 4s 6d a week for the rent. AW would recall awakening at night to hear the rumble of the mangle being turned. In his biographical book *Fellwanderer* (1966), he was to recall his young days in an area of flickering gas-lamps, hot-potato carts, fish-and-chip shops, public houses and Saturday matinees at a cinema known—not without justification—as 'the flea pit'.

He had developed a love of hill-climbing as a small boy, loving high and lonely places and conceiving an ambition to climb Everest and die on its summit. Whenever possible, stimulated by the availability of maps, he escaped from the Blackburn millscape to high and lonely places. His other diversion was to stand on the terraces at the football ground to watch Blackburn Rovers. He remained a Rovers fan to the end. Leaving school at the age of thirteen, he had made little progress along the way of learning. Then, realising that if he wanted to 'get on' he must pass examinations, he studied English language and literature, commenting, 'This made me a stickler for the correct use of language. I found myself criticising the way that people spoke and sought to use the words correctly myself.'

Alfred Wainwright surveys the scene.

AW's first job on leaving school was a modest role in local government. He was a bespectacled young man, taciturn by nature, with ginger hair. As a white-collar worker, training in a modest role at Blackburn Town Hall, he acquired a love of words and figures. Their use was to become a means of making a good living and also an art of combined writing and drawing. His love of fish and chips endured to the end of his life.

Ruth, whom he married, was a weaver. They met—as did many townsfolk—at chapel. Ere long, a son was born and a house was found in a new estate, far enough away from the Town Hall for AW to find it convenient to drop in on his mother at lunch-time. I never met Ruth but have a feeling that AW was off-hand with her. Most of the Wainwright family liked Ruth, but relations between her and AW became strained, and they parted. Years later, interviewed by Sue Lawley on the radio for *Desert Island Discs*, he was asked if his fell-walking had any effect on his domestic life. He replied, in an unkindly fashion, that his wife and the dog had gone for a walk one night—and he had not seen them since.

His Lakeland fell-walking career had actually begun in 1930, when he and a cousin, while holidaymaking, walked up Orrest Head, above Windermere, and saw elements of the English Lake District for the first time. There was a view across Windermere to the Coniston Fells, and it appeared to him as heaven on earth. AW switched from Blackburn to the finance department of Kendal Borough Council, and when I first met him he had a responsible job in a second-storey office at the Town Hall. He eventually became Borough Treasurer.

As editor of *Cumbria* magazine I was keen to interview him. AW, broad and bespectacled, gave virtually a wordless interview. After a period of Quaker-like silence he agreed to my idea that I should write down some questions, send them to him and he would provide the answers. This arrangement worked. In his office, he eventually opened a drawer of his desk to reveal a few line drawings of Lakeland fells, some of which had been glimpsed when, aged twenty-three, he developed a passion for fell-climbing.

His visits to parts of the Lake District had been via bus from Kendal. If he stayed at a bed-and-breakfast house for the night the charge was usually about 4*s*. His first Lakeland sorties saw him clad in everyday clothes, with stout shoes on his feet. He carried a raincoat. Subsequently he wore a good jacket over his everyday clothes and had some ex-army nailed boots on to his feet. He became a loner in his fell-top world, being lost in his own thoughts, not suffering fools gladly, speaking, Quaker-style, only when he was moved by the spirit. AW had no need for a rucksack. He pocketed in an old raincoat his pipe and tobacco, his few provisions and the camera he used to photograph the fells in detail. Later, photo-prints were the basis of his fine drawings. He did not even carry a compass, marking his Ordnance Survey maps and then copying them in a way that would not be tolerated today without authority and payment of a fee.

In 1938, when war clouds were gathering, AW undertook a walk along the Pennines with his shadow as a sole companion. He penned an account of the jaunt, entitling it *A Pennine Journey*. It lay in a drawer for almost fifty years before publication. On his long walk he had overnight accommodation in a farmhouse or inn.

The Wainwright book entitled *Pennine Way Companion* achieved fame. In it he offered a free pint to any walker who had genuinely done the whole route; it was so popular that this reward had to be reduced to half a pint. When AW had assessed the route, he travelled light, his small rucksack being virtually empty. He could have managed quite well without it.

Among the contents were three maps, 'the one in use being carried in [his] pocket'. He had 'a toothbrush and a safety razor, a bottle of Indian ink and a pen, pencils and a rubber and a few postcards … All told, the entire contents … would weigh less than 2 pounds, so that [he] was free to square [his] shoulders and stride out as quickly as [he] pleased'. Ascending a highspot, he would take photographic 'snaps' and make notes.

On the evening of November 9, 1952, relaxing at his Kendal home, he drew the first page of what would turn out to be a series of guide books, prose and pictures being related to Lakeland fells. They were penned meticulously, using Indian ink. At evening-tide, occupying a spare bedroom at home, with a cat for company, he created in line the distinctive pen-and-ink impressions of individual fells and noted the best ways to climb them. Progress was at the rate of a composed page per day. He was diverted from his mission only by his cat and the television series *Coronation Street*, which reminded him of his upbringing in urban Lancashire. By July 1953 he had created a host of pages. He disliked the ruggedness of the line-ends—they were not 'justified', to use a printer's term. He scrapped these pages and did the work again, making the pages neater and tidier.

Henry Marshall, the Kendal librarian, had his name printed as publisher, below that of the author, on the title page of the first of what would become an outstanding and distinctive series of guide books. Known as Wainwrights, they would describe 214 fells. My most significant occasion relating to Wainwright was when Harry Firth, printer at the *Westmorland Gazette* in Kendal, arrived in the *Dalesman* office in the village of Clapham. Harry supervised the printing of *Cumbria* magazine, which I edited. He laid on my desk a slender parcel, wrapped in newsprint. It was the original work—drawings and miniscule writing—relating to the first of the Wainwright guides to the Lakeland fells. Every word, line and dot had been jotted down by Wainwright.

The first of his *Pictorial Guides*, costing £900 to produce, had a muted reception, but his special vision of the Lakeland fells, his pawky humour and inventive skill, had soon elevated him to cult status. The work developed on such a scale that eventually, when I called at the printing works to put *Cumbria* magazine to bed, I would pass down a gorge between cliffs of white paper that had been earmarked for the works of AW.

In the years from 1952 to 1965 he compiled seven pictorial guides. His style did not change. AW remarked, 'If I was starting all over again, I would not change a thing.' I compiled lists of Wainwright's chief likes and dislikes:

Likes: Betty, his wife; skylines, pipe and tobacco, fish and chips, maps, well-used boots, Blackburn Rovers, *Coronation Street*, Old Kendal, Cats (not so keen on dogs), yet more fish and chips. He enjoyed visits to the cinema, one of his favourite films being *Oklahoma*, and especially the song 'O What a Beautiful Morning'.

Dislikes: Gaelic names for Scottish mountains; sociable fell-walkers, passing the time of day with school parties (one 'good morning' had to do), car seat belts, cruelty to animals, bad grammar and most places south of Blackburn.

It became an occupation of many fell-walkers to 'do the Wainwrights' and climb all the peaks highlighted in his extraordinary seven-volume *Pictorial Guide to the Lakeland Fells*. Visiting all 214 has become a common form of 'peak bagging'. The first to complete the challenge was Alan Heaton, in an incredible time of nine days and sixteen hours, in 1985. The youngest was a boy of six in 2008! For the vast majority it has been a more leisurely pursuit. The Geriatric Blunderers eventually climbed them all, as well as completing the Coast-to-Coast walk from St Bees Head, in the west, to Robin Hood's Bay, on the Yorkshire Coast. Having made a ruler mark across the map between the two points, AW spent a year on the project. He worked at a section until the maps, information and text were compiled to his satisfaction; he then moved to the next stage. Completed in 1972, the Coast-to-Coast was to become even more popular than his Pennine Way, the theme of another Wainwright handbook.

Part of my training for tackling the western half of the Coast-to-Coast walk, in 1994, was eating fish and chips at a shop in Kirkby Stephen, which is roughly halfway along the route and had a framed photo of Wainwright—who used the term 'chip shop'. On *Desert Island Discs* he asked, plaintively, 'Will there be a chippy on the island?'

Like me, Wainwright was 'partial' to this deep-fried, crisp, hot and golden fare. My regard for fish and chips dates back to the 1930s, when it was possible to get a generous helping of both for thruppence! In the days before vegetable oils were used, hunks of 'dripping' floated in the pans like mini-icebergs. In a BBC television series in which Wainwright's companion was Eric Robson, they munched their way through a memorable sequence in which they dined on fried cod and chipped taties.

We began the western part of the Coast-to-Coast expedition at St Bees, wading ankle-deep into the Irish Sea to collect pebbles—one each—that would eventually be tossed into the North Sea. We followed an eroded path at the edge of the redstone sea cliffs, being vocally mocked by herring gulls. Fulmar petrels had their flight sustained by an updraught. There were shrubs on the cliff. A yellow hammer uttered a ditty that sounded like 'a little bit of bread and no cheese'. Wainwright's directions led us from on a long drag from Cleator to the summit of Dent at 1,100 feet. There followed a sharp descent into Nannycatch Gate. We passed close to a stone circle that looked modern and was presumably a Victorian sham. At Ennerdale Bridge we dined and slept in a detached house with a shrubby, cat-haunted garden.

We chatted with our host about the Coast-to-Coast Walk. There were titters when we heard of some foreign but English-speaking visitors who used, for direction, a coffee-table version of Mr Wainwright's Coast-to-Coast book, two-thirds of the illustrations being coloured pictures.

On the following day there was a bright golden haze in the meadows, and the fells that stood around Ennerdale were in various shades of blue and grey. Our path led along the western shore of the lake, which the construction of a dam had turned into a large and pretty stretch of water. A passing raven appeared to salute us by flicking momentarily on to its back. The gee-whiz country dominated by Gable and Pillar was near at hand, but first we had to slog through Forestry Commission plantations. It was appropriate to include a visit to Haystacks, via Scarth Gap, to pay homage to the founder of the walk we were now enjoying. His ashes were scattered beside Innominate Tarn, a name implying 'The Nameless One'. AW's first visit had been during a trip from Blackburn in 1930; it became his favourite hill. He had told Eric Robson, his companion in many television programmes, 'I shall end up here.' Someone would carry his cremated remains and deposit them close to Innominate Tarn:

> …where the water gently laps the gravely shore and the heather blooms and Pillar and Gable keep unfailing watch … And if you, dear reader, should get a bit of grit to your boot as you are crossing Haystacks in years to come, please treat it with respect. It might be me!

A notion that Innominate Tarn should be named after Wainwright was turned down. The name Innominate means nameless, and he detested the idea of messing around with the Ordnance map. Dear Haystacks—as he once addressed it—was described by him as 'a quiet, lonely place'. It was not always kind to him. Among the BBC films taken

The 'Geriatric Blunderers' at Innominate Tarn, the location where Alfred Wainwright's ashes were scattered.

Wainwright with Betty, his wife.

for a series based on his fell-walking career was a sequence 'shot' in wind and rain near the tarn. It was dull and windy; the Lakeland sky was weeping for him! He remarked that if he wandered on Haystacks for hour after hour he would always find something different to look at—small crags and sinuous paths. An eighteenth-century cartographer wrote over Haystacks the words 'here eagles build'. The hill is not especially noted for its bird life. AW recorded the name as being Norse, meaning 'High Rocks', and had heard a fanciful story that the fell was so-named because of the scattered tors on the summit. They resembled stacks of hay in a summer meadow.

My last glimpse of AW was when he and Betty called to see me on the eve of my retirement from the editorship of *Cumbria* magazine. His eyesight had declined and now he walked haltingly. Strands of grey hair overlapped his coat collar. They called to see me at my office in the village of Clapham in 1987; they came to wish me well. He was hefty, around 6 feet in height, and she was small and lean. I photographed them in the Dalesman yard. He smiled at the camera, one arm around the diminutive Betty.

I gathered from his wife that AW was not very sociable when he left the house. When he was indoors he was unable to cope with practical jobs. It was a dull, damp day. As an old dalesman I knew would have remarked, 'T'day looks as if it had bin up all neet.' Betty went for a walk, remarking, 'I'll call back in half an hour.' AW spent five minutes stoking up his pipe before saying, after a Quaker-like pause, 'I'm sure we'll find something interesting to say to each other.' We were soon heading down Memory Lane. There was a publishing bond; we had been allowed to carry specimen Wainwright pages in each of our magazines, which had a combined worldwide circulation of around 90,000 copies. He was grateful for the publicity at a time when sales were sluggish. Seven pictorial guides were compiled for his pleasure in the years from 1952 to 1965, both years inclusive, as a buff advertisement form would have noted.

Betty drove us to the nearby village of Austwick, where we dined at the Gamecock Inn. Eating in public was not an experience he enjoyed. With Betty at the wheel, we returned to Clapham. AW detested seatbelts, so he sprawled himself in the back, where they were yet to be required to be worn. On the by-pass, I suggested to Betty that she parked up and let me finish my journey on foot. There are three ways in to the village, yet she contrived to stop midway between two of them. I bade my farewell, clambered out and looked back at the cloth-capped, pipe-smoking frame of AW in the back window. Then they were gone. A sudden, sharp shower persuaded me to complete my journey at jogging pace.

His vision deteriorated in his old age. Lakeland became a blur, but his mind remained alert and, happily for him, he could close his eyes and picture whatever scenes took his fancy. He was also fond of recalling that fell-walking had brought him into contact with sheep. He felt sorry for them and preferred what he regarded as these dignified animals to many people he met on his walks. After his death, in 1991, the Geriatric Blunderers, would occasionally visit Betty, his small, bright, hospitable second wife, who continued to live in a spacious bungalow situated in Burnside, not very far from Kendal, the town with strong Wainwright connections. She became our honorary president.

The marriage of AW to Betty had lasted for rather more than twenty years. When Betty had first become associated with AW he had red hair. She called him Red, a second reason being that 'red' was the second part of Alfred, his Christian name. At the bungalow I saw Wainwright in framed photographs. A corner of a spare room held some of his walking gear. Ninety per cent of our talk was about the Lancashire Lad who had become widely known for his excursions on the Lakeland fells and, now and again, on mountains in the north-west of Scotland.

On the stonework beside a window in Buttermere church is a plaque commemorating Wainwright—artist, writer and compiler of a notable set of Lakeland guides. Through the window, in clear weather, Haystacks might be viewed. I was among those who attended the inaugural meeting of the Wainwright Society, held at Ambleside Youth Hostel on a November day in 2002. In the chosen room were fans from the far corners of the land. Eric Robson provided the ideal chairman (and was, indeed, elected so). His utterances were short, pertinent and often amusing. We heard of a farmer objecting to AW directing people across three of his fields 'to a green lane'—this led to the gate being painted black!

Robert Walker,
a Wonderful Man

Born in 1709, Robert Walker was the youngest and weakest of a large family. Later he became known as 'Wonderful Walker', a nickname relating to his industrious nature and variety of skills. Robert, born in the Duddon Valley, was 'bred a scholar'. He became a teacher at Buttermere, marrying a lass who had a dowry of £40. The money was never used.

He settled down as parson and schoolteacher at Seathwaite in 1736. He and his family developed the art of 'living off nowt'. He had a busy life; it was said of him that his seat was within the rails of the altar and the communion table was his desk. While children were repeating their lessons by his side, he worked a spinning wheel. His life fascinated Wordsworth to the extent that he described Walker's busy life in two of his literary works. He also noted that Walker had a single luxury—this was a woollen covering to the family pew. The covering had been spun by the hands of Wonderful Walker. By day, he tended to teach, garden, attend to a few cows and sheep that lived on the fellside and any other task that needed to be completed. Clerical duties were carried out at night.

The Walkers had eight children. They were trained to keep their eyes on hedges and pluck from them any strands of wool that adorned them. Each evening, in a tiny cottage, the wool, termed 'hodden grey', was spun into clothing for the family while a member of the family read aloud, usually from the Bible. Walker bore any surplus wool on his back and trudged over a hill to the nearest market.

As curate, Walker received £5 a year. The amount rose to £50 during his long spell of service. Wonderful Walker died in 1802. He was ninety-two years of age, being in his sixtieth year as curate at Seathwaite. His frugal wife had predeceased him by a few months.

Hugh Walpole,
Author of *Herries Chronicle*

Hugh Walpole was a bachelor who bestrode two worlds—literary and social. He was feted at his home in London and discovered Lakeland when he was forty years of age. While staying in Keswick in the autumn of 1923 he overheard a hotelier remark that a house called Brackenburn, overlooking Derwentwater, was on the market. Walpole acquired the property and, with it, the necessary peace and quietness for his penmanship.

Brackenburn, his 'little paradise on Catbells', was imposing, and fitted a delightful scene. Nearby was a bracken-clad hillside. Becks tumbled down towards the lawn. Walpole encouraged visitors—among them was J. B. Priestley, the novelist and playwright known informally as 'Jolly Jack'. He was photographed with Walpole in the grounds. These two highly-regarded writers had collaborated in *Farthing Hall*, a novel based on an exchange of letters. Among other notable visitors was W. H. Auden, a simple and jolly soul who 'did not make [Walpole] feel a silly, worn-out old man'.

Walpole created *Herries Chronicle*, a good and folksy novel set in the eighteenth-century world and featuring a striking character named Rogue Herries. Borrowdale and its surrounding fells became Herries Country. Walpole was to write four associated novels, named *Rogue Herries, Judith Paris, The Fortress* and *Vanessa*. References were made to the most vital happenings in England between the years 1730 and 1932, and the novels were eventually presented in one volume entitled *Herries Chronicle*—1,488 pages of quality fiction, set against descriptions of Lakeland life and scenery the author had grown to love.

At Brackenburn, Walpole had arranged for an imposing building to be constructed at a lower level than the house and beside a road that separated it from a wooded area beside Derwentwater. His new property consisted of a large garage with a second storey forming a quiet and spacious study where his writing might be undertaken. It also became a repository for 30,000 books.

At the house itself, a long mirror was set above a grand fireplace in the lounge, enabling Walpole, when seated before it, to see a panoramic reflection of Derwentwater. He might enjoy its colours and moods without turning his head. If the kitchen tap was left running for a short time, the water was clear and sparkling, like wine brought up from a cellar; it had flowed from the heart of the fell that lay behind the house.

The Herries Country created by Walpole took in Borrowdale and also its surrounding fells. At Grange-in-Borrowdale, a graceful double-bridge spans the Derwent, a bridge that Walpole had in mind when he was writing about Old Mrs Wilson. Suspected of being a witch, she had been tossed from the bridge to her death through drowning. Stockley Bridge, which arches itself over the beck on the route from Seathwaite to Sty Head, saw an encounter between David Herries and a pedlar with a 'sharp bright face' who said he was the Devil. Walpole placed an inn at Wasdale Head, describing the premises as 'a small place … smelling of food, ale, dung, human unwashed bodies'. In Herries' time, no such inn existed.

My last tour of the Herries Country was as part of an autumn course on Lakeland writers and artists that was organised by Abbot Hall, a Methodist guest house overlooking Morecambe Bay. I had the leading role. We travelled to Keswick by luxury coach; a mini-bus shuffle had been arranged from there to Watendlath, which Walpole knew, loved and used as a literary setting. It was an autumn day, touched by the lean forefinger of winter. The air was dull, moist and chilling. Derwentwater was gleaming. Walpole wrote about the lake on a day when 'the water whispered with the soft splash of oars'. We took to the hills at Ashness, crossed the celebrated little bridge, and then stopped briefly at the Surprise View of Derwentwater and Skiddaw. Eventually we reached Watendlath, in the *Judith Paris* section of National Trust country, recalling an old-time rift that Walpole devised between two local families, each of whom claimed they were living in Judith's house. Walpole had diplomatically mentioned that he had no specific local building in mind, though it is clear from his description which property was intended.

Sir Rupert Hart-Davis, who was Walpole's friend and biographer, confirmed for me an impression of Walpole as a man who needed each of his worlds—London and Lakeland—and who was bored if he remained in one of them for too long. He needed excitement and the adulation of London so he switched from one to another.

Walpole, in all the seventeen years he owned Brackenburn, never lived there for more than five weeks at a stretch. He died at the age of fifty-seven; a Celtic cross marks his grave in St John's churchyard in Keswick. Walpole had chosen his last resting-place on a springtime day, when the churchyard was 'scattered with snowdrops'. He had regarded the view from the churchyard as superb. A collection of Walpole manuscripts and memorabilia associated with the writer may be seen in Keswick's Fitz Park Museum.

John Wesley and Methodism

John Wesley made the first of many visits to Lakeland in 1751. He jotted some details in his diary; the next day he and his companions rode to Ambleside, and on a Saturday, 'over more than Welsh mountains to Whitehaven'. Eight years later he was back, paying a visit to colliers at Whitehaven and then preaching in the Vale of Lorton, near Cockermouth. People who heard him 'found God to be a God both of the hills and valleys, and nowhere more present than in the mountains of Cumberland'.

Wesley, who was no great lover of hills, implied that God might be found even in Lorton, where one might least expect to find evidence of His great mercy. He made an alternative approach to Whitehaven, crossing Morecambe Bay at low tide. Wesley paid his last visit to Kendal in 1788—he had celebrated his eighty-fifth birthday.

In the early days of Methodism, converts met in their own homes. So-called Class Meetings were organised for prayer and Bible study. Methodism initially appealed to working class folk to whom the established Church paid little regard. A man who attended a meeting at Kendal joined the Methodist cause, remarking to his class leader during a meeting that 'people say I'm cracked'. The class leader closed his eyes, bowed his head and remarked, 'Let us pray. Oh, Lord, crack a few more—there's plenty of work for them to do down here.'

Jonty Wilson, a Shoer of Horses

The Lune Valley, painted by Turner with colour and described by Ruskin in words, is a gem that is situated twixt the Lake District and Yorkshire. Jonty Wilson, blacksmith at Kirkby Lonsdale, knew it especially well. As a horseman, he had ridden on every green track and bridleway, remarking, 'There can be very few areas in these islands to compare with the dales and fells of Westmorland.'

Jonty was unhappy at the passing of what he called 'oral traditions'. 'Crafts, skills, tools and dialect words have become obsolete and meaningless now,' he said. When I first met Jonty, at the smithy in the part of town known as Fairbank, he was eighty-two years of age. A native of Low Biggins, in the same parish, he had been a blacksmith for almost seventy years. He mentioned that in the 1920s there were still many working horses to be seen. Men spoke about them with an enthusiasm now reserved for motor vehicles. Blacksmith shops were numerous. Attention to a horse was proportionately cheaper than it is to a modern car.

Jonty said that in his young days a smithy was like parliament—a place where men discussed horses, hunting, crops, sport, trade, politics, religion and local scandal. Every facet of rural life was chewed over in the smithy. Men sat on benches round the fire as their fore-elders had done for generations. There was, naturally, much talk about horses; Jonty had lived into a time when what he knew as the horse-world and also old husbandry had disappeared. Said he, 'They've passed into the limbo of history.'

Jonty was fourteen years old when, in 1907, he began work as an indentured apprentice. He was paid 2s 6d a week. His workplace, a smithy on the capacious Underley estate, was presided over by a hulking but normally genial man named Ted Read. Ted weighed 16.5 stone and was a noted rugby player for Kendal. When Jonty met him, Ted estimated that over the years he had shod about 55,000 horses. During Army service in France, he helped a local smith to shoe a draft-ox.

The Underley estate of Lord Henry was vast, employing 177 people. There were thirty-two gardeners, thirty-four foresters, fourteen gamekeepers, plus painters, masons, joiners, blacksmiths and a small army of employees who worked in the big house. Sixteen men attended to eighty-two stabled horses, seventeen of which were hunters. Four Russian stallions were kept simply for drawing the carriage used by the family and friends during the London season. Three post horses operated a 'shuttle service' between Underley Hall and the town, collecting (among other things) the Royal Mail.

Jonty was greatly aware that the industrial revolution changed the lives of people in town and city but existence on the land remained heart-breaking and back-breaking:

When I was young I seemed to live in a world of men who were old. It was a time of unrest. Fit young men emigrated to Canada, Australia and other colonies, where prospects were brighter.

Jonty had witnessed a line of six men, with long-bladed scythes, working across a field of oats. 'I saw youngsters making the bands for the sheaves, women gathering up grain and tying the bands and men setting the sheaves into stooks.' Men with flails threshed the grain on a barn floor. It was a time when the voice of a corncrake might be heard—and rabbits would be seen running for shelter.

Jonty's father was fussy about drinking milk. Some farmers had TB-infected cattle that, nonetheless, represented cash on the hoof at a time when money was scarce. Father told his family that they mustn't drink cow's milk. He bought some goats. Jonty did not like goat's milk but was assured it was never infected by TB. Mother told Jonty, in later life, that the expenditure on food per head each day must not exceed one and threequarter pence or they would be in debt.

Jonty not only remembered the old days—he took up photography, part-time, in 1908, recording them. A quarter-plate camera had cost five shillings. Sensitised plates—thruppence each—might be purchased from a local chemist. Fifty sheets of photo-printing paper might be bought for 11d. His family home had no running water so he had recourse to the nearby River Lune when he wished to wash the fixative from newly-developed plates. He would prop a wet plate against a boulder and collect it an hour or so later. Happily, the plates kept their quality. He laughed at the recollection of disbelief on the faces of two burly refuse collectors as they approached what they believed to be an average dustbin. Their arms were nearly wrenched out of their sockets by the concealed weight of the massed photographic plates.

At about the time of the First World War, the number of people employed on Underley estate was in decline. Many had 'joined up' and some were never to return. Rising costs meant that not as many people could be employed. Jonty reckoned that the wage bill for 177 people in the old days would be about the same as that for half a dozen men at the time we chatted. Jonty performed jobs which are now almost forgotten. One of them was frost-sharpening the shoes of horses so that they might keep their feet on slippery roads in winter. Roused from his bed at 3 a.m., he helped other smiths to attend to a large number of horses on the night of one of the county balls, a splendid occasion that attracted the nobility of the region.

Jonty grew up in a world that seemed half-full of horses. The streets of Kirkby Lonsdale had piles of dung; a man was employed to regularly sweep them up. The largest assembly of horses in the town was at the Royal Hotel. Sixty-two fine animals occupied extensive stabling. On market day, farmers left their horses here. Visitors passing through the district who stopped for a meal had their horses rested and fed.

Devil's Bridge at Kirkby Lonsdale, 1801—for many, a symbolic entry into the Lake District.

Jonty reckoned there had been more changes in national life in the last 100 years than in the previous 1,000 years.

The maintenance of a horse was proportionately cheaper than it was when Jonty and I met for the umpteenth time in 1975. In the 1920s, having a horse shod with four new iron shoes cost 9s 6d. A 'remove'—taking shoes off, dressing the feet and replacing the shoes— was done for 3s 6d. A thrifty farmer ensured that horse shoes lasted longer in summer by fitting *cogs* (blunt metal pegs). In winter, when the roads were *slape* (slippery), the blacksmith fitted 'sharps' into the holes on a shoe so that the horse might keep on its feet on such a surface.

When I chatted with Jonty, he invariably mentioned the Galloway Gate, an early version of the M6. The Gate extended for some 130 miles from lowland Lancashire through eastern Lakeland and into south-west Scotland. 'Galloway' was the name given to a cob, seen commonly on a farm, where it was 'maid of all work'. The route was used by the drovers of cattle—100,000 head of cattle—with groups of other beasts making a yearly pilgrimage.

When Jonty was a very old man, I took him for a car journey along the twisting, narrow roads of the Lune valley. He had a tale to recount about every mile of the way. Jonty's grave is in the churchyard extension. To me, his spirit is everywhere in the town where he lived for more than ninety years.

40

William Wordsworth, the Real Man

William Wordsworth and his cronies were familiar with an approach to the Lake District via a crossing of low-tide Morecambe Bay. He had a fanciful idea that an outstanding view of the Lakes was to be had by sitting on a cloud and looking downwards on fells and lakes. The idea has been updated in recent times by various films that have captured the beauty of the Lake District from the air, often accompanied by enchanting music.

The spirit of William Wordsworth pervades the Lake District. Thomas De Quincey calculated that the Wordsworthian legs 'must have traversed a distance of 175 to 180,000 English miles'. This best-known Lakeland poet (1770–1850) was born in Cockermouth. His father was land agent to Sir James Lowther. Spending his boyhood in Hawkshead and Colthouse, young Wordsworth noticed that bunches of unfledged ravens were suspended at Hawkshead churchyard, a reward of 'so much a head' being given to 'the adventurous destroyer'. To Wordsworth, the effort of seeking ravens was exhilarating. He would recall in verse:

Oh! When I have hung
Above the raven's nest by knots of grass
And half inch fissures in the slippery rock,
But ill-sustained, and almost (so it seemed)
Suspended by the blast that blew amain,
Shouldering the naked crag.

Wordsworth had enjoyed lively schooldays at Hawkshead, climbing, skating, fishing, nutting, rowing on the lakes and rambling on the fells. In France, he had witnessed aspects of the Revolution. Visiting Germany, he saw and met a goodly number of stimulating thinkers. In 1799, when he returned to his native district as a young poet, he must have been aware of a revolutionary fervour in Europe that was sweeping away the old-time classicism. For him, a dazzling new world began on the doorstep of Dove Cottage at Grasmere. He responded emotionally to the grandeur of the scene and also commonplace sights and sounds. Problems with the Scots had been solved; peace prevailed in the border counties. The price of wool had risen but rents remained comparatively low. There was spare cash, so a period of re-building in stone had begun.

A drawing of a thoughtful William Wordsworth.

He set up house in Westmorland. He and his friends would become known as The Lake Poets, a term derived from 'The Lake School', which had been used (mockingly) by a writer in the *Edinburgh Review* of 1807. Wordsworth's writing style was simple and perspective. Being himself of 'statesman stock', he knew and loved the men of the dales. The man who became the Lake District's most famous poet joyfully met them when he could, observing:

> ...towards the head of these Dales was found a perfect Republic of Shepherds and Agriculturalists, among whom the plough of each man was confined to the maintenance of his own family, or to the occasional accommodation of his neighbour.

Two or three cattle furnished each family with milk and cheese.

The chapel was the only edifice that presided over the dwellings:

> Neither high-born nobleman, knight or esquire was here but many of these humble sons of the hills had a consciousness that the land on which they walked over—and tilled—had for more than five hundred years been possessed by men of their name and blood...

Long legs carried Wordsworth over vast distances, up hill, down dale, with time to pause and look around. A memorable day was when, in the company of his sister Dorothy, he glimpsed flowers in bloom by Ullswater. Nature had shrugged off winter, and snowdrops were on display. A shore by Ullswater was enlivened by the fresh yellow of daffodils which, to William Wordsworth and his sister Dorothy, 'danced' in the breeze.

> *I wandered lonely as a cloud*
> *That floats on high o'er vales and hills,*
> *When all at once I saw a crowd,*
> *A host of golden daffodils;*
> *Beside the lake, beneath the trees,*
> *Fluttering and dancing in the breeze.*

They were words that would become widely familiar. Creativity was a combined operation. His wife and sister were involved in verse relating to 'golden daffodils' in April 1802. Dorothy, his sister, confided in her journal, 'When we were in the woods beyond Gowbarrow Park we saw a few daffodils close to the waterside.' This is in the area where Aira Force juts out into Ullswater. These daffodils would be of the small, wild variety. 'They tossed and reeled and danced and seemed as if they verily laughed with the wind.' William transformed the prose into splendid verse. The first version of the poem was compiled two years later and published four years after the event described. He quelled the storm but left a breeze:

Continuous as the stars that shine
And twinkle on the milky way,
They stretched in never-ending line
Along the margin of the bay:
Ten thousand saw I at a glance,
Tossing their heads in sprightly dance.

This verse was added between the publication of the first version in 1807 and the final version of 1815. It was Mary, the wife of William, who suggested a thought that would be enshrined in the lines: 'They flash upon that inward eye/ Which is the bliss of solitude'. William was not writing a school textbook; what matter if he exaggerated a little, claiming to see 'a host of dancing daffodils'? Two lines later, there were 'Ten thousand dancing in the breeze'.

The daffodil throng was compared with 'the stars that shine/And twinkle on the milky way...' In his day, the concept of the Milky Way would be novel. In the third verse of the final version, he exchanged the word 'laughing' with the archaic 'jocund':

The waves beside them danced, but they
Out-did the sparkling waves in glee:
A poet could not but be gay.
In such a jocund company:
I gazed—and gazed—but little thought
What wealth the show to me had brought.

Wordsworth was not content merely to write about daffodils. He planted some, adorning the tract of hillside land he bought at Rydal in 1826 for Dora, his daughter. This tract became known as Dora's Field, and, ere long, daffodils jostled with narcissi. The last verse of the daffodil poem might be played to organ accompaniment:

For oft, when on my couch I lie
In vacant or in pensive mood,
They flash upon that inward eye
Which is the bliss of solitude,
And then my heart with pleasure fills,
And dances with the daffodils.

The Wordsworths settled in Dove Cottage at Grasmere in December 1799. Grasmere was not the first choice; W. P. Morris, in *The Records of Patterdale* (1903), declared that William Wordsworth would have made his home in Patterdale had a great flood not frightened him. He and his sister Dorothy lived for a short time at Broad How. It had been his intention to build a little mansion on some rocks close by. One morning, after a heavy night's rain, seeing the rocks were little islands, 'he there and then betook himself away, and sought for Grasmere'.

Dove Cottage, Grasmere.

They had travelled from Kendal by post-chaise, and *en route* undoubtedly watched the interplay of light on snow-covered hills. It was almost dark when the chaise lurched its way along a rough road into Grasmere Vale. They were put down outside Dove Cottage at 5 p.m. Molly Fisher, who was to be their daily help, greeted them in a stone-flagged room and ensured they would be warm by providing a blazing fire in the hearth.

Dove Cottage became a monument to plain living and high thinking. Wordsworth was to write:

> *And now, 'tis mine, perchance for life, dear Vale*
> *Beloved Grasmere (let the wandering streams*
> *Take up, the cloud-capt hills repeat, the name).*
> *One of thy lowly dwellings is my home.*

With its rough white walls and diamond-paned windows, the Cottage was peaceful enough during the eight years that the Wordsworths called it home. Years before that it had been The Dove and Olive Bough, one of the many country inns. When Grasmere was only a cluster of buildings near the lake, Dove Cottage was known as Town End.

The Wordsworths were grateful for the warmth of the fire when they reached Dove Cottage in 1799. My first memory of the place—in a hot, almost stuffy afternoon in the summer of 1957—was of the delicious, tingling coolness of the old rooms. The cool atmosphere was in part influenced by the tax on window space—an idiotic and unhygienic scheme that the government had introduced to augment its revenue.

When I was being shown through its cool rooms I half-expected to interrupt William at his work or come face-to-face with Dorothy. She both ran the cottage and helped her brother with his inspired composition. I gathered that the Wordsworths had to be careful with the use of water. It was drawn from a well they had dug in the garden.

Canon Rawnsley (1903) quoted an old servant of the Wordsworths who indicated that William was fond of a good dinner at times, 'if you could get him to it ... It was poddish for t'breakfast and a bit o' mutton to t'dinner'. At night, more poddish, 'with a bit o' cheese 'appen to end up with'.

At the end of the eighteenth century, fewer than 300 people were living in the hamlets of Grasmere Vale. The church is very much as it was when he penned *The Excursion*:

> *Not raised in nice proportion was the pile,*
> *But large and massy; for duration built;*
> *With pillars crowded, and a roof upheld*
> *By naked rafters, intricately crossed,*
> *Like leafless underboughs in some thick wood,*
> *All withered by the depth of shade above.*

Grasmere was peaceful and pastoral, the home of unsophisticated but proud and fiercely independent farmers who were known as 'statesmen'. Their ranks were being rapidly thinned by social changes. Grasmere had no castle, no large hall, no squire nor other important landowner.

When the vale was marshy and uninviting, the tracks used by travellers were on high ground. A turnpike was constructed at Grasmere about 1770; there was a toll bar on the Raise. The new road crossed White Moss Common to the south of Grasmere vale. In his verse, Wordsworth was moved emotionally by the commonplace—and, indeed, not just by daffodils:

> *Thanks to the human heart by which we live;*
> *Thanks to its tenderness, its joys and fears;*
> *To me, the meanest flower that blows can give*
> *Thoughts that do often lie too deep for tears.*

The Rainbow features in his 'Intimations of Immortality':

> *My heart leaps up when I behold*
> *A rainbow in the sky:*
> *So was it when my life began;*
> *So it is now I am a man;*
> *So be it when I shall grow old,*
> *Or let me die!*
> *The Child is Father of the Man;*
> *And I could wish my days to be*
> *Bound each to each by natural piety.*

The Wordsworths were fond of visiting Penrith, which had been the home town of each of their parents and the place where they attended a dame school run by Ann Birkett. Another pupil—Mary Hutchinson—was to become William's wife in 1802. On a sunny day in 1808 the Wordsworths vacated Dove Cottage and headed for Allan Bank. By now he had both a wife and a family. Dorothy must have suffered from great sadness at the thought of what Dove Cottage had been.

Some of Wordsworth's grandest lines were prompted during a journey to France. He beheld London from Westminster Bridge:

> *Earth has not anything to show more fair:*
> *Dull would he be of soul who could pass by*
> *A sight so touching in its majesty:*
> *This City now doth like a garment wear*
> *The beauty of the morning, silent, bare.*
> *Ships, towers, domes, theatres and temples lie*
> *Open unto the fields, and to the sky,*
> *All bright and glittering in the smokeless air…*

Wordsworth's grave in Grasmere churchyard, situated in a family plot and marked by a simple tombstone, has a grand setting. The village where he spent much of his life is surrounded by fells he loved. His verse lives on. An imaginative thought of what one might see when sitting on a cloud, looking down on the hills, was referred to in modern times when a DVD was produced. Tracts of Lakeland were filmed from a helicopter; some sensitive music caught the spirit of the region in what Wordsworth had achieved imaginarily in prose and verse.

Mardale, a Lost Village

I drove to high-lying Shap, had coffee and a buttered scone in Mrs Bell's café, and looked at some photographs of Old Mardale that adorned the walls. Mardale had been drowned by Manchester Waterworks. The water of a conversion from lake to reservoir emerged from the city taps.

I first saw Haweswater almost forty years before. Wordsworth, in his *Guide to the Lakes* (fifth edition, 1835) described the reservoir as 'a lesser Ullswater'. He was pleased that 'it remains undefiled by the intrusion of bad taste'. Alfred Wainwright wrote a piece about Mardale Green when it had lost its life by drowning. 'All that is left are ghosts.'

The fells had been tinged blue-grey by mist. In the foreground were irregularly shaped fields which lay on the landscape like a patchwork quilt. Then my eyes focused on the dam that had transformed Haweswater, a natural lake, into a reservoir—a water cistern for Manchester. Lapping water had displaced the local farming community. The conversion had taken place at a time when the district needed employment and money. Farming was in the doldrums in the 1920s and 1930s.

Three huge oil engines had generated electricity for the construction work. Concrete was conveyed to the dam on overhead buckets. I chatted with an old-time member of the Manchester City Council. His first glimpse of Haweswater had been in the early 1890s, when he was cycling with a friend, making their way from Manchester to Carlisle. They left their bikes at the top end of Longsleddale and strode over Gatesgarth to see the lake.

I followed a road that lay on a ledge blasted from living rock. It extended from Naddle Gate to the dalehead. The explosives used by the road-makers would have disturbed the peacefulness of Naddle Forest, a resort of red squirrels and red deer. Nature had put a green-dressing on the sores. The deer returned behind a screen of new growth.

A large and attractive hotel was built. Guests were able to watch red squirrels cavorting on the deciduous trees and, from the front terrace, in the days of which I write, they might have seen a golden eagle. England's first nesting pair of eagles for a century or two chose to nest on a ledge in one of the recesses of Mardale. I watched a pair of peregrine falcons scolding the larger birds.

The peak time for visiting Haweswater would be in a drought year; a fall in the water level might reveal traces of a scattering of farms with a church, school and hotel. A writer in *The Manchester Guardian* in 1918 wrote: 'Four or five farmhouses lie here and there among the lower meadows; a tiny church, plain-built in a Puritan century,

Fell ponies near Haweswater.

squats amid its yews.' The church, dedicated to the Holy Trinity, was one of the smallest in Lakeland. It had seating for only fifty people and, towards the end of its life, served a total population of seventy. 'The only touches of modernity were the schoolhouse and vicarage…' Worshippers were summoned by the clanging of a bell that was made in 1825. John Turner, of Mardale Green, was the first burial, the year being 1729. Prior to this, a dead person was conveyed by being strapped to the back of a pony or horse, up the zig-zags of what became known as the Corpse Road, which crests at 1,656 feet and leads to Swindale and Shap.

In his novel *The Shadow of a Crime*, Hall Caine recorded the death and internment of a wicked man. He died in Mardale and was buried at Shap, the coffin being strapped to the back of a horse. When the weather became thundery, the horse bolted. It roamed to and fro across undulating Swindale Common for three long months. Eventually, the horse was recaptured. As indicated, the corpse was laid to rest at Shap.

Edward Baines, an early tourist who travelled on horseback, arrived in Mardale in pre-reservoir days and had to rouse 'mine host' of the Dun Bull from his bed. Baines described Mardale as 'a lively, fertile and beautiful valley'. There were very few habitations. Baines attained the summit of High Street—a broad tract of land covered with short grass. When horse-racing took place here an alternative name was Racecourse Hill. My first ascent of High Street was in the company of Dick Hilton, who had been grievously wounded when he trod on a landmine during the Italian campaign of the Second World War. Dick recovered his health and made up for the loss of one leg with a wooden substitute. We walked on to High Street via Blea Tarn and I can still clearly recall the *thwack, thump* of boot and wooden leg as Dick followed me.

In summer, Haweswater has its busy and quiet sides. The last time I sauntered along the footpath west of the water, I was *en route* from St Bees and Robin Hood's Bay on the celebrated Coast-to-Coast route devised by Wainwright. The last time I went this way, in the summer of 1993, a buzzard was wheeling and mewing over the crags. An astonishingly fat stoat bounded from one patch of bracken to another. The path broke from the cover of trees, giving me a stunning view of Naddle Forest, beyond a lake that was gleaming in sunlight. High fells were huddling around the head of the water.

Epilogue

I was extremely fortunate to have discovered the Lake District back in the 1950s, a time in my life when I had plenty of opportunity ahead of me to get to know it. I loved to learn about the rich personalities of the famous—people like William Wordsworth—but it is the 'natives' who have provided endless fascination. The local folk of the Lakes, such as the craftsmen, the shepherds and the daleheaders at the top of valleys have given me endless interviews that have increased my knowledge of subjects and allowed me to become an authority on, for instance, the Herdwick Sheep. I have visited many of the traditional shows and come to understand much about the Lakeland folk. They can be set in their ways but always keen to talk about their lives and seasonal jobs such as haymaking and lambing. Native-born folk also find pleasure in recalling customs that were recounted to them by their ancestors; historians note in fine detail facts and figures of the old days. Some folk gave me a unique insight into the lives of the famous, such as the old chap who lived near Beatrix Potter and was her shepherd. A way of life has changed appreciably with the passing of time. I witnessed the last great phase in the area's history before the arrival of 'second homes' and the modern age.

My love of the area has extended beyond research connected with work. My travels over the fells with the 'Geriatric Blunderers' have opened up high Lakeland and its glorious mountains. Those joyful days have long since gone, but memories have been recorded in our walk-by-walk accounts which describe in detail each and every trip. Bob, Stan, Colin and I, along with our patient wives, have enjoyed an annual meal for years over at Cockermouth, with a stop for a cuppa and toast at Ambleside. Sadly, Freda, my dear wife, passed away eight years ago. She gave me every chance to indulge my love for Lakeland and I will always be grateful to her for that.

I am sure that because of advancing old age this will be my last book on this beautiful part of the world, but I am happy that the subject appropriately conforms to the 'people before places' adage that has dominated my life and given me so much pleasure.